HOW CHURCHES FIGHT POVERTY:

60 successful local projects .

Elma L. Greenwood

FRIENDSHIP PRESS   NEW YORK

Second Printing—May 1968

LIBRARY OF CONGRESS CATALOG CARD NUMBER: 67-30302

COPYRIGHT © 1967 BY FRIENDSHIP PRESS, INC.
PRINTED IN THE UNITED STATES OF AMERICA

In the distance I saw
  Something moving
    Which looked like an animal . . .
As I came closer I saw
  It was
    A man . . .
When we came face to face
  I recognized
    My brother . . .

—Author Unknown

CONTENTS

Introduction

J. Edward Carothers, long-time local pastor and now Associate General Secretary of the Methodist Board of Missions and chairman of the National Council of Churches' Anti-Poverty Task Force, says: "It is very likely that local churches will determine whether the war against poverty will end in victory or defeat for the nation."

This seemed like an overstatement, and when I first heard it I was inclined to be skeptical. After 5 months of observing local churches and church-connected groups engaged in anti-poverty activities I now find myself much closer to agreement with Dr. Carothers' assessment.

This shift in attitude came gradually as I spent from June through October 1966 on an assignment from the National Council of Churches' Anti-Poverty Task Force, studying religiously related groups in action on the poverty war front. The purpose of the study was to show, through brief accounts of a selected list of effective, church-related, anti-poverty projects, the "what," "who" and most importantly "how" with which they began and are functioning.

My journeys extended into urban, suburban and rural areas from New England to Hawaii, from Georgia to Oregon, and covered approximately 60 successfully functioning groups. The projects studied are mostly Protestant, though they also include Roman Catholic and Jewish groups. Many combine all 3 faiths and represent activities of the major religious forces of the community. Recommendations for projects to be studied came from specialists on the NCC Anti-Poverty Task Force, from executives of state and city councils of churches and from National Council of Churches field staff members in many localities.

This book presents the results of this rare opportunity to observe the contribution of thousands of religiously committed people, working through agencies and programs of practically every known variety, toward the goal of eliminating grinding, inexcusable poverty in the world's most affluent nation.

What in general did these five months of watching, listening, talking and questioning show? Though the study was not about poverty as such, or—except incidentally—about the government's War on Poverty, I was constantly impressed, as I listened to the story of the first two years of the churches' struggle, with two little-recognized but universal features of the total anti-poverty effort.

The first factor was the vast difference between our approach to this struggle and to the shooting wars we are used to engaging in. In the attack on poverty, not only have we had an enemy of a wholly different stripe, size and locale; we have also had an unprecedented lack of preparation for attacking him. In "military" terms we entered this contest against man's oldest and toughest foe with no war department (prepared in advance to direct the fighting), no army (staffed, trained and ready to do the fighting) and no stockpile of tested weapons (ready for instant use in combat).

Because money was being committed, the new "command" was expected to produce results from the day the struggle began. With the enemy entrenched in practically every hamlet, town and city, the hastily mobilized "army" had to do battle not only in such widely varying terrains as inner-city neighborhoods and rural crossroads; it also had to start fighting in as many of them as possible, all at once.

So rapid and high-pressured have the developments been since the "war" was declared that we recall only with difficulty the unpreparedness of the nation even for the facts of the existence of poverty in its midst, dramatically revealed in Michael Harrington's *The Other America* as recently as March 1962. Churchmen taking part in the National Council of Churches' Consultation on "The Churches and Persistent Pockets of Poverty" in January 1962 now find it hard to realize how suddenly revealing at that time was the word brought by Dr. Oscar Ornati (just beginning his history-making Twentieth Century Fund study of poverty in the USA) that we as a nation had during the 1950's reached the "cross-over point" from scarcity to abundance, where the American economy finally became "productive enough to do away with poverty." This and other "discoveries" at that consultation caused the participants to stress, for the first time, in their statement to the churches that "because poverty is no longer necessary, it is ethically intolerable."

We must remind ourselves also that the fact of the nation's economic ability to eliminate poverty was only brought forward officially as recently as January 1964 by the President's Council of Economic Advisors. Its moral implications were then expressed for the nation as a whole by President Johnson: "Today for the first time in our history we have the power to strike away the barriers to full participation in our society. Having the power, we have the duty. . . ." (Message to Congress, August 1964).

All anti-poverty battlers have had to proceed the hard way, learning as they fought. In spite of the unparalleled tempo, complications and widespread unpreparedness of the total undertaking, little quarter for either reflection or mistakes has been granted by a general public inclined from the beginning to be opposed, grudging or skeptical.

A second factor, which has only recently begun to be recognized, is the whole new "mix" of human and institutional interaction—public-private, governmental-nongovernmental, profit-nonprofit, social-economic-political-religious—that has come about, particularly in local communities, as a result of structural flexibility under OEO procedures. This permissive approach, including the introduction of a whole new third force—the people in poverty themselves—has added to the general confusion and acrimony of this first learning period. The national plan, however, located responsibility in every community for developing its own mixture of program emphasis, local leadership and work force to meet its unique poverty needs, conditions and resources. Credit must be given to the overall planners for recognizing at the outset that no other approach could possibly have mobilized the exceptional combination of forces that have swung into action against poverty and its causes in so many local communities.

Twice in one week, as I have been writing these lines, both a former and the present U. S. Secretary of Health, Education and Welfare have referred, for the first time to my knowledge, to the surprising failure of the whole nation to sense the revolutionary nature of many happenings in the spectrum of organized activity involved in the attack on poverty. Dr. Arthur S. Flemming, HEW Secretary in President Eisenhower's cabinet and recently elected President of the National Council of Churches, indicated his belief that "very few people in this country today realize the extent of the revolution that has taken place in these (internal social, economic and political) areas in the last five years." Dr. John N. Gardner, the present Secretary, has said that the nation cannot solve *any* of its significant national problems without the help of the private sector. "I don't think many Americans understand the extent to which much of recent legislation dealing with health, education, poverty, the cities and so on devolves *initiative and operating responsibility* to the grass roots. . . . " (*The New York Times,* April 2, 1967)

"Creative federalism" is the term now being used to describe some features of the new phenomenon of federally financed, locally conducted activities, greatly expanded by the poverty war. Studying at close range the anti-poverty activities of many church groups, I became acutely aware that not only the governmental-nongovernmental interaction but the merged activity between different private organizations and institutions with an extraordinary variety of interests, backgrounds and sources of support constitute a degree of person-with-person cooperation across institutional lines that would have been inconceivable five years ago. Whatever the future of the poverty war as such, its first two-year demonstration of how *all* elements of a community can be brought into working cooperation around a common (nonmilitary!) cause has been not only a revolutionary, but a hopefully enduring, experience. To lose this momentum now, when many communities and leaders have just learned what can be done and how, would be not only an immediate, but an historic, tragedy.

In the center of this new amalgam, functioning with an unprecedented assembly of partners, I found churches, church groups and church people. Perhaps the most common characteristic of all the projects visited was the extent to which each one differed from every other one—since each one presented a one-of-a-kind combination of 1) the pressing need to be met, 2) the nature, philosophy and genius of its leadership, and 3) the resources in people, funds, facilities and working allies in the community being served.

Among the few general things that can be said about the churches in relation to the anti-poverty struggle the study seems to document four:

1. *The churches are in action on the poverty front,* in a quantity and a depth that have proved amazing to me and to many others. In the vast new alignment of community forces set in motion by the poverty war, religious groups have had a prominent, often determining, part. They have participated as one of the many segments in the "creative federalism" supported by public funds; many have also moved out on their own, relying on combinations of congregational, denominational, interchurch, interreligious or other private groups and resources. With due allowance for what one observer has called "the full immensity of what is not being done," I believe what has been done by the churches during these beginning years of the anti-poverty struggle has provided a demonstration of the possibilities of "creative Christianity" seldom, if ever, duplicated in the churches' history.

2. *Church groups have distinct contributions to make in the anti-poverty struggle.* In addition to being regarded by many—deservedly

or undeservedly—as "reservoirs of the outpouring spirit," church groups or agencies have as a rule been freer: to pioneer in methods of outreach; to test various approaches and pass them on to public bodies; to emphasize full, decision-making participation by the people living in poverty; and to conduct or encourage programs in neighborhood or community organization independent of sometimes hampering public support.

3. *The churches are singularly well-equipped with resources to fulfill their role.* These include a concerned leadership, volunteer services, facilities and money, all of a quality or quantity seldom duplicated by other nongovernmental institutions. Wherever there is a *will* to get into action, any church group can count on substantial assets already at hand as it searches for the *way.*

4. *The churches have developed a corps of experienced operating leadership among their project directors.* The churches as a whole should not only support them more generously (which goes without saying!) but should also recognize and use them more widely in developing overall strategies and applying specialized techniques in local areas and communities. Clearly the project operators who have struggled through these first trial-and-error years have learned a lot; and if I am any judge *they have just begun to fight!*

While writing this account I realize that by the time it is read, what is described as current will be at least a year old. In this era of life on the move "we can no longer stand still but must be swept into the mainstream of living." What one year's rushing mainstream of change may do to the nationwide struggle against poverty, and to the rays of hope with which it has begun to penetrate the darkness, is of course uncertain. Yet there is one thing I feel safe in predicting— the people I met and talked to, who have fought through this first stretch on the front lines where the "bombs" of neglect and exploitation have worked their havoc for centuries, will not leave the poverty battlefields unless we in the churches fail in the behind-the-lines support on which they must depend.

There is an inside story of every family and every institution. A significant item in the inside-the-church-family story came frequently into view during this study. I refer to the pervading influence of the religious groups, singly or most potently in combination, which has played a highly significant part in these first years of anti-poverty "structuring" in most American communities. While there are instances in which this influence has not always been as enlightened, disinterested or self-forgetting as might be hoped, my observation has been that these religiously based people have provided and continue to be

11

counted on for a special quality of service in directing, enriching, often salvaging the whole anti-poverty effort in many localities. This influence has often been exercised by the organizers and directors of the anti-poverty programs described in these chapters.

In the Washington National Cathedral is a collection of statues dedicated "to saints and heroes of all Christian traditions." While I know that a saint or a hero is the last thing any of these harried, round-the-clock, anti-poverty pioneers would call themselves, I do believe they are making history—distinguished, God-and-man-appreciated history—both in the family of the church and on its behalf in the world.

This book supplements the informative materials already available through the statements and countrywide anti-poverty programs of the National Council of Churches and through the special emphases on poverty of the National Council's Departments of United Church Women and Education for Mission. The word "effective" in my assignment was interpreted to mean a project that was ongoing, well-organized and successfully functioning, as measured by knowledgeable workers on national or local levels. "Church-related" meant that there was a definable connection with one or more religious bodies of whatever size, location or faith. In all statements and programs of the National Council of Churches the term "anti-poverty" refers to the total effort of the nation—both governmental and nongovernmental. This study includes many activities supported in whole or in part by the federal government's War on Poverty funds; it also includes many independently functioning and supported activities.

Obviously anyone making a "study" can cause it to come up with preconceived results. This is what I did, seeking by definition to describe a sampling of anti-poverty projects that have "worked." No attempt has been made to assess how representative the projects are, either of the anti-poverty effort as a whole or even of all the church-sponsored programs. In a situation where much information reaching public attention tends to stress the "con" side of the anti-poverty effort, this presentation seeks a "pro" perspective. "I am so glad to learn that something positive is happening," has been the most frequent reaction to the story of my summer's experiences.

Each project has been described in terms of its development and functioning up to the time of my contact with it, which was at some point between June and November 1966. Any later developments are indicated in footnotes. The facts and general presentation about each project have been verified by the persons originally interviewed; expressions of judgment or personal references are my own.

Fortunately we already have in Lyle E. Schaller's *The Churches' War on Poverty* (Abingdon, 1967) a comprehensive view of the history and development of the churches' participation in the national anti-poverty effort, as well as a pro and con discussion of many questions raised by that involvement. Dr. Schaller's book, together with numerous publications available from the National Council of Churches' Anti-Poverty Task Force, gives details of the national denominational, interdenominational and more recently interchurch and interreligious programs. The NCC Task Force programs are currently directed by Rev. Larold K. Schulz, its Anti-Poverty Co-ordinator.

The projects here are illustrations, presented with as much detail as time and pages have allowed, of the activities which other writers have outlined more sweepingly.

1 Job Training and Placement

Able-bodied poor people today are saying, "Give us jobs, and we will solve our problems." Quite contrary to popular myths, anti-poverty workers report from wide experience that desire for work at a living wage far outruns interest in guaranteed income devices.

Recognition that employment at adequate wages is the number one antidote to poverty has led church people to turn enthusiastically to projects for training or retraining men and women in current work skills and for helping them find use for such skills in today's labor market. Outstanding examples of church-initiated, sponsored and/or operated job training and placement projects are described in this chapter. Three factors characterize each of them: *first,* an obvious need not being met in other ways; *second,* vision, faith and determination of a small corps of economic realists willing to take and maintain leadership; *third,* an outcome, through what one director has called "a great partnership between government, industry and the people," that has well surpassed the aims of their church-connected sponsors.

OPPORTUNITIES INDUSTRIALIZATION CENTER, PHILADELPHIA, PENNSYLVANIA

"Whosoever will let him come." This invitation of our Lord, which has given spiritual sustenance to his followers through the centuries, has now been extended to the giving of physical and material help to thousands of people in poverty in Philadelphia. This practical help comes through the wide-open door of the Opportunities Industrialization Center (OIC), a job training and placement enterprise.

Whereas in many programs there is a tendency to screen people out, "in OIC everybody is screened in," said Rev. Leon H. Sullivan, pastor of Zion Baptist Church at the corner of Broad and Venango

Streets. Leon Sullivan, himself a Negro reared in poverty in a small West Virginia community, is the "dreamer and doer" whose foresight, leadership, and tireless effort have brought into being one of the nation's most significant human resource development programs. The OIC is designed not only to give new job skills to people greatly needing them, but also "to inspire them with hope, confidence, and a new way of looking at themselves and at life."

In organizing and operating OIC Mr. Sullivan has been supported throughout by the pastors and many members of 400 Negro churches in Philadelphia. "Just as God helps those who help themselves, I believe Americans will join in helping those who strive to help themselves," he said.

The self-help philosophy has also enabled Leon Sullivan to enlist the support of business, educational and philanthropic leaders across the nation. His "community-forged weapon against poverty and degradation" operated for some time with private funds. It has since expanded considerably with support from the OEO and from the Departments of Labor and of Health, Education and Welfare. OIC's success has caused it to be duplicated in many other cities, again through both public and private funding. "The most important step came when government joined with industry and philanthropy in a great partnership with the people in this program," Mr. Sullivan stated.

Stress on Economics. Leon Sullivan has from the outset emphasized economic means to achieve economic opportunity. Ten years ago he convinced fellow Negro pastors, and through them many church members, that the one economic "means" available to all of them was their purchasing power. Through a program of "selective patronage" they were able to bring corporation after corporation to agree to abandon restrictive employment policies. When this undertaking revealed a lack of job skills and experience among the minority group community, the churches decided to pool their own and other resources and train their workers themselves.

A door-to-door canvass of the Negro area raised $102,000 in cash and equipment, and the Ford Foundation added grants totaling $200,000. In an abandoned jailhouse, refurbished with the help of enthusiastic volunteers, the OIC opened for business in February 1964.

How the Centers Have Operated. The OIC screens in everyone coming to its doors by a process of "intake" counseling. Each applicant is referred immediately to a counselor who, through testing if necessary, learns about his or her needs and potentialities. Well over

15

90 percent of the applicants find a starting point in the OIC program; and after acceptance each trainee is assigned to a permanent counselor, who helps him select a field for training. In the few cases of obvious unemployability, information is given as to where other help is available.

Twenty-seven recruiters go into the streets, the homes and the bars, explaining what the Center has to offer those who need its kind of opportunity, but who sometimes need help to see it. "Once we can reach them on their own level," said an experienced recruiter, "we can usually unwind their twisted minds. We are frequently amazed at how quickly the man or boy with roughest exterior will respond to the atmosphere of hard-headed, but warm-hearted, interest he encounters once he comes to the Center."

Each trainee starts with the "feeder" program, where all phases of prevocational training prepare him for referral to other centers of OIC for specialized training. The time required for a trainee to advance through the feeder classes varies, but averages 6 to 8 weeks.

The feeder functions from 8:30 A.M. to 10 P.M., Monday through Friday. It covers introduction to job categories, job-finding techniques, minority history, grooming and hygiene, civil service exam preparation, English as a foreign language, consumer education, remedial reading and basic adult education. Other courses provide specialized training such as communication skills (concentrating on reading and writing difficulties), computational skills (mathematics from simple arithmetic to trigonometry) and attitude orientation.

After completing the feeder program the trainee has a choice between 25 job training areas, with training given in 4 locations across the city. The job areas include: restaurant practices (from waitress to chief cook and manager), teletype, drafting, power sewing, laboratory technicians, machine shop (including repair and maintenance), sheet metal, electronics and electronic assembly, secretarial science including typing and office machine operation, merchandising-marketing, real estate sales preparation, IBM key punch, small business management, laundry and dry cleaning, plumbing, heating and air conditioning, brick masonry, commercial art and various printing operations.

Rev. William A. Hill, official visitors' guide, dramatized the day-to-day outcome of the training courses with the story of Mrs. W. The sole support of two children and currently "on relief," Mrs. W. had developed exceptional skill with the power sewing machine. At 4 o'clock one afternoon her instructor told her she had been selected to fill a "special request" job in a men's garment firm, to begin the next day. "How can I ever do it?" Mrs. W. was reluctant even to try.

"We think you can do it," her teacher assured her, though she knew that very few women are ever employed to work on men's clothing. Mrs. W. was finally persuaded to report for the new job the next morning. "She has adjusted very smoothly," her teacher told us, "though she is the only woman and the only Negro in that large shop. We knew she could do the work, but I knew also that if she heard about this in advance and had time to think about its difficulties, she wouldn't have had the courage to try it."

The OIC training is related to the newest industrial techniques and processes, with every area operating under guidance of a technical advisory committee which checks and rechecks the curriculum. Through these committees the industries involved have given much of the necessary, up-to-date equipment used and also provided new employment opportunities for the trainees. "The pay-off," said Mr. Sullivan, "is that when given the opportunity, the OIC trainee has proved his ability to do the job. Once our trainees were lucky if they had jobs sweeping around the machines. Now they operate them."

Adult Education Program. The newest venture for extending the OIC self-help idea into the community is a special adult "armchair education" program. A volunteer teacher is provided for every group of 8 or more adults who come together in a neighbor's home. In this relaxed situation, discussion centers around consumer education, citizenship principles and problems of the immediate community. Many are reached who would or could not come to the Center school. It also serves to introduce many to OIC feeder and training programs.

The adult education project is a direct responsibility of the Community Organization Department. This sprightly branch keeps in various degrees of involvement over 1,000 volunteers from the churches, the neighborhoods and other areas of the city.

In OIC's two years of operation more than 3,000 men and women, many of whom were unemployed and all of whom were underemployed, have been trained and placed in productive jobs in Philadelphia's offices, stores and industries. Some 1,600 others continue in various stages of training. More than 35 percent of OIC trainees come from the relief rolls, and better than 95 percent represent persons or families living in poverty.

"We have discovered that lack of job preparation comes in technicolor," said Mr. Sullivan. Though the Philadelphia program began in the colored community through the efforts of the colored community to help itself, scores of white men and women are now enrolled in OIC and hundreds are on the waiting list of more than 6,000 people.

17

National Outreach Through OIC Institute. The best indication of OIC's extraordinary success is the OIC Institute, an independent agency supported by public funds from OEO and the Department of Labor Manpower Office, plus private contributions and a foundation grant. The Institute provides information and technical services without charge to spread the OIC idea across the nation and even to other countries, Mr. Elmer Young, administrative assistant to Mr. Sullivan at Zion Baptist Church, explained to me.

The September 12, 1966 *OEO News Summary* reports that the Opportunities Industrialization Center will be extended to 8 other cities. Through the cooperative efforts and support of the OEO and the Departments of Labor and of Health, Education and Welfare, a $5 million program is establishing comprehensive manpower centers in Harrisburg, Pennsylvania; Oklahoma City, Oklahoma; Menlo Park, California; Little Rock, Arkansas; Erie, Pennsylvania; Roanoke, Virginia; Seattle, Washington; and Washington, D.C.

Through the Institute at least 40 other cities are taking the first steps toward launching an OIC program. The key to success, Leon Sullivan feels, is OIC's community roots. "It is important to raise some of the funds from the community," he says. "The people then have a stake in their centers and they won't let them die."

OIC pays no training allowances. All classes are free, and effort is made to help trainees get part-time jobs while training, where this is needed, "but the people who come have to want to be here." The program has an amazingly low dropout rate, with the greatest inducement for staying being the nearly 90 percent promise of a well-paying job.

Church Backing and Involvement. "God helping us—we shall succeed," says the brochure that explains OIC's purpose, objectives, procedures and hopes. The signal success of the program testifies to the reality of God's help in the face of what the skeptics insisted were insurmountable difficulties and "impractical" realities. "A demonstration of faith in action" OIC is called by its religion-oriented governing board.

From its earliest days the movement that culminated in OIC has been a distinctly church-related activity. In every description the "dime-to-dollar" contributions of parishioners in the 4,000-member Zion Baptist and many other Negro churches are given credit for making those beginnings possible. What this support means in proportion to the community's financial "assets" is indicated by one account of the area as a "nightmarish section of six city wards of squalid

18

streets and rotting red-brick tenements, packed with 270,000 people and faced with appalling want and social decay."

Without question the OIC project has become one of the most notable of the many church-based anti-poverty undertakings in the nation. The fact should be both reiterated and emphasized that OIC is a lasting monument to the vision, devotion, and undaunted faith in their fellowmen of the Negro churches in Philadelphia—and, through them, in many other urban centers throughout the nation.

TRI-FAITH EMPLOYMENT PROJECT, CHICAGO, ILLINOIS

"The people who come through this employment office may lack many advantages but ambition isn't one of them," said Father Michael Dempsey, chairman of the Neighborhood Advisory Council of the Lawndale-for-Better-Jobs Employment Center.

The Center, located in the basement of Our Lady of Lourdes School, had just "jubilized" over placing Mrs. H., an unemployed mother of 2 children, in the 1,000th job filled since the Center had opened less than a year before.

This experimental neighborhood office, concentrating on placement of needy unemployed or underemployed workers, opened its doors in October 1965 in the heart of North Lawndale, an impoverished area of Chicago, with funds provided by the Chicago Committee on Urban Opportunity. By October 1966 the Center had found permanent, full-time work for 1,071 job seekers "at salaries averaging $2.15 per hour for men and $1.60 per hour for women." A checkup near the end of the period showed that 83 percent of those placed were still working.

The success of this experiment led the tri-faith Chicago Conference on Religion and Race to propose a citywide network of similar job placement centers. Something of a speed record was set, in a) getting prompt approval of the plan by the "establishments" of the three faiths (involved in the CCRR), b) enlisting cooperation of churches in communities selected as center sites, c) drafting a request proposal for OEO funding, and d) seeing it through to receipt of a grant of $136,000. This was accomplished in time for the placement program known as the Tri-Faith Employment Project to open in July 1966, with 7 centers operating in churches or storefronts in areas of greatest need across Chicago.

Each Center is staffed by 5 qualified local residents. Each one works in cooperation with the Chicago Committee on Urban Opportunity and can turn for advice and job development to the city's business and industrial leaders who are active members of the Chicago Conference on Religion and Race. Whole-hearted cooperation of church members

19

in the Center areas is helping to identify the hard-core unemployed. At the Centers their needs are sympathetically reviewed and practical answers are given. In addition to placing many applicants directly into waiting jobs, the Center staffs are also alert to get those needing training into MDTA Training Centers often in the same localities.

By early October 1966 the Centers, during a little more than 2 months, had matched up better than 700 applicants with work opportunities—many of them the best chance at honest, decent-paying employment the job-starved person had ever had.[1]

This project has been initiated, promoted and operated by the combined religious forces of Chicago. Its process could readily be duplicated in other urban centers, large or small, where the only truly indigenous and stable elements in a slum community are usually its religious institutions.

NATIONAL COMMITTEE ON HOUSEHOLD EMPLOYMENT (NCHE)

Another job-centered program of a different type is being developed by the National Committee on Household Employment (NCHE), a nonprofit corporation uniting the efforts of many national organizations, including the National Council of Catholic Women, National Council of Jewish Women, the Church Women United, and the Woman's Division of The Methodist Church.

The purpose of the NCHE is to provide leadership in promoting and establishing standards for household work; improve the economic and social status of household workers; stimulate job development and training programs; and serve as liaison with government, private and community agencies.

The NCHE is sponsoring a series of 6 pilot training projects in various parts of the country, establishing Community Committees on Household Employment and developing discussion materials. Local members of the incorporating groups will be brought together in the training areas for volunteer service in counseling and encouraging domestic workers to take part in the training. The local committees will also engage in efforts to change community attitudes, develop and practice high employment standards, investigate local practices and make their voices heard on behalf of adequate wages, including state minimum wage laws.

United Church Women of Arlington and northern Virginia recently participated with other women of the area in the first local meeting

[1] A more recent report shows that, since the Centers were funded in July 1966, 1,600 firms had placed job orders and accepted 3,100 applicants referred by the Centers.

to consider the problems, needs and attitudes related to domestic employment in that section and to endorse the plan for a local training institute. The Christian Social Relations Section of the Methodist Woman's Division endorsed the NCHE program at its January 1967 meeting and called for Methodist women to become informed about the program and unite with others to organize local Household Employment Committees.

"We should not make the poor bear the burden of our homes," said Father Geno Baroni, Secretary of the Roman Catholic Archdiocese of Washington. "Women in household work are on the bottom of the economic ladder, they have no minimum wage guarantee, no retirement programs, nor are they adequately compensated for the work they do."

If accepted and implemented by churchwomen across the nation in anything like the spirit they have shown in other anti-poverty activities, this program to upgrade both the ability and the earnings of domestic workers could provide a strategic advance for one of the neediest groups on the anti-poverty battlefront.

OTHER TRAINING AND PLACEMENT PROGRAMS

Roman Catholic groups in particular have specialized in training for better economic opportunity. Outstanding have been the projects of the Michigan Catholic Conference at Lansing (for settled migrants and Cuban refugees) and at Mt. Pleasant (for Indians from the Chippewa reservation). Soon after the MDT Act was passed, the bishops were persuaded, in the face of a rapid build-up of hard-core unemployment in the area, to take the unprecedented step of using the corporate status of the Michigan Catholic Conference to contract with the U.S. Department of Labor for funding of one of the first of the job training programs called for under the Act. While the conference has continued to serve as sponsor of the project, it has had no further connection with its operation, which is carried on by a full-time professionally trained staff.

The program includes a pretraining cycle, basic education (as needed) and classroom or on-the-job training in 6 job-skill areas— machine operators, auto mechanics, clerk-typists, custodians, cooks or cashiers. A full complement of counseling, health and family services is also provided. In a little more than a year of operation, the number of boys and girls, men and women given the training was over 2,500 of many races, nationalities, and degrees of need and educational levels.

Another widely recognized Catholic sponsored program is STAR,

Inc.—Systematic Training and Redevelopment—a large-scale project initiated by the Natchez-Jackson Diocese of Mississippi, and financed, in August 1965, by grants totaling nearly $7 million from both OEO and the U.S. Department of Labor. With participation of Catholics and Protestants, Negro and white, on its policy board, it has conducted a rare kind of interreligious, interracial operation on behalf of displaced farm hands from the plantations of this area of the deep South.

Predating the efforts of both Protestant and Catholic agencies in vocational and work adjustment are the Jewish Vocational Service programs in many cities. These have been providing vocational counseling, job placement, group guidance and rehabilitation assistance to the physically handicapped, the older workers and others in need of special help for 25 years and more. Concentrating at first on services to the Jewish community, many programs have recently expanded, with government help, and now extend their services to all people in the community.

An example of such a program is the Jewish Employment and Vocational Service of Philadelphia, whose Work Adjustment Center is a nonsectarian, interracial agency functioning with grants from the Labor and HEW Departments. It offers a short-term, paid-employment experience for otherwise unemployable youths and adults—the mentally retarded, emotionally disturbed, disabled, chronically ill, "sociopathic or inadequate persons"—which includes vocational evaluation, personal and work adjustment training, sheltered employment, individual and group counseling and family casework services.

Related more directly to the poverty program is the project known as COPE (Career Oriented Preparation for Employment), operated by the Jewish Vocational Service of Newark, New Jersey, under sponsorship of the United Community Fund and the United Community Corporation (official OEO agency). It seeks to open new paths to vocational opportunity for disadvantaged youth between 16 and 21. By successfully enlisting the cooperation of 50 social, civic and religious agencies as trainer-employers, COPE during its first 6 months placed and supervised the training of 400 boys and girls in subprofessional jobs such as teachers' and nurses' aides and community organizer assistants, as well as in clerical and maintenance operations. They work either part or full time at $1.25 an hour on assignments lasting from 6 to 9 months. A special feature is the advance and followup counseling provided by COPE's experienced vocational guidance staff.

A number of training and employment programs are also described in other chapters, including programs for migrant farm workers (Chapter 9), older teens and young adults (Chapter 3) and rural area residents (Chapter 6).

Why have religious groups been able to achieve such success in these various kinds of vocational efforts? Some of the reasons seem to come from the nature of religious groups in contrast with other groups in our society, others simply from the fact that "this is the way a religious group has of doing things."

In job training and placement, as in many other economic activities, both employers and employees usually respect the economically "neutral" position of the religious leader or group. Thus a church-based project has, by its nature, a substantial head start in reaching out to both groups needed to make any job-related program a working reality. Increasing emphasis on on-the-job training has also required more and more cooperation from the nation's industrial leaders, many of whom have become personally interested in training programs as a result of their contact with church-initiated projects.

For projects like these to have permanent results, the approach to those in greatest need of help has to be highly personal, as nearly as possible the one-to-one relationship. Such an approach must be used: *first*, in the recruiting, where prospective trainees are not just notified but sought out man-for-man, on street corners, in bars or in crap games; *second*, in the training, especially where progression is based on individual attainment rather than on a fixed instruction period; and *finally*, in the follow-up, where the continuing contact is again not only persistent but warmly personal. The person-to-person approach seems to be made most easily and naturally by religiously oriented people or groups.

Perhaps most important of all is the belief, held in common by many church-connected pioneers in job training and placement efforts, that most people in poverty are eager to grasp any *promising* opportunity to lift themselves out of that condition. This confidence is well expressed in the "working philosophy" of the Tri-Faith Employment Project:

"We believe that the vast majority of inner-city residents will, if given the chance, become self-supporting, productive citizens. The high rate of unemployment found in inner-city communities can be attributed to the exacting needs of today's labor market, to racial and ethnic discrimination and to a system of mis-education rather than to the attitudes and aspirations of the people who are chronically out of work."

23

Referring to how this philosophy works in practice, Monroe B. Sullivan, Tri-Faith's project coordinator, notes that "each week between 400 and 500 unemployed or ill-paid men and women confirm us in our belief. . . . They do not come to us looking for charity. They come because they want to work."

There seems, in fact, to be little backing among the operators of church-related employment projects for the popular notion that people are poor because they don't want to work.

2 The Youngest Victims of Poverty

"I didn't know there were boys like me who have never had a book," says a pensive 5-year-old pictured in a recent ad for children's books. I venture to say many adults would not have known or believed it either up to 3 years ago.

About that time the poverty "warriors" decided to start a human resource development program with the youngest children. As they began urging them out from the homes of "disadvantaged" people across the land, the advantaged adult world was amazed to learn how literally barren life could be for 3- and 4-year-olds in "the other America."

Effort has been made to remedy the situation through a network of preschool programs for children from families in poverty. These have been large and small projects, supported by public or private funds or combinations of the two. Most comprehensive has been Head Start, developed by the OEO.

The care and education of children have long been a primary concern of the churches, beginning with religious nurture of the children of church members. Care of children beyond the membership circle has also long been provided by church-supported orphanages and more recently by children's homes, hospitals and other child-care institutions. Still greater shock was experienced, therefore, by many people of "concerned Christian conscience" to learn how universal has been the failure of these institutions—fine as many of them are in themselves —to meet the needs of that large company of God's children unfortunate enough to be born in the poorest slum areas, urban and rural, across the nation.

Church groups, agencies and members, however, have been among the first to respond to this critical situation once it was revealed, by becoming promoters of the anti-poverty-inspired preschool movement.

THE PRE-SCHOOL COUNCIL OF NEWARK, NEW JERSEY

"It's too early to see whether they'll turn out to be commercial artists or gym teachers," said Mrs. B., the assistant teacher, as she guided me through or around clusters of busy 4-year-olds.

Some gave final touches to the morning's finger painting or a last bounce to the big rubber ball in delayed answer to the "clean up" call, which had sounded as we came in. After this, an appetizing hot meal, a brief nap or rest period and reluctant leave-taking rounded out the morning half of the daily schedule at Mt. Calvary Baptist Pre-School Center in Newark, New Jersey.

This Center is operated by a nonprofit citizens organization, the Newark Pre-School Council, Inc., in the first *year-round* preschool education program funded by the OEO. The project began in September 1965 with a budget of $2.3 million. As its first year's sessions ended in June 1966 it was providing daily classes for more than 2,000 4-year-olds in the areas of need across the city.

How It Began. "It all started with a phone call from Dr. Leontyne Young," said Rev. Kim Jefferson, executive secretary of the Greater Newark Council of Churches. As director of the Children's Service Association and as an active member of the Council of Churches' Social Welfare Department, Dr. Young had been wrestling with a growing concern of both groups, to initiate some citywide program for disadvantaged children. The phone call enlisted Kim Jefferson, already widely known for leadership in organizing Newark's citywide OEO program, and together they assembled a small group of citizens, who decided that a sponsoring group of individuals (not organizations) should be formed. This plan was eagerly accepted by the Community Mobilization Center (an information and referral agency in the area to be served, of which Mrs. Rebecca Andrade was director) and by other influential civic and social agencies. At a larger meeting in January 1965, 40 individuals, associated with these organizations, voted to form the Newark Pre-School Council, Inc. By April a request for funding went to the local OEO agency and was finally approved in September 1965.

In the Pre-School Council, membership is open to all persons resident in Newark and to others interested in preschool education in the city. Its board of directors includes 4 ex officio members from government agencies, 39 to 55 from the parents or area boards and 12 to 15 members at large, representing churches, social work agencies, child care groups, teacher training institutions, business, labor and civil rights groups.

With support from local religious and other community sources to supplement its OEO funds, the Council has sought to offer a program to place the less-advantaged children of Newark on an equal footing with others with greater economic and educational opportunities.

The preschool program started with 67 classrooms in 47 donated facilities, 34 furnished by churches or synagogues. The number grew to 46 during the year, including 42 Protestant, 2 Roman Catholic and 2 Jewish organizations, which volunteered the use of church school rooms, basements or whatever space could meet the stringent health and safety requirements. Many, operating on deficit budgets themselves, assumed the added expenses of lighting, heating and custodial services.

Staff. The supervisory staff included an executive director, a program director, 7 field coordinators and 17 unit supervisors. Each classroom was staffed with a training teacher, a teacher-in-training and a teacher's assistant. Through an intensive recruiting program the full staff of field coordinators, unit supervisors, classroom teachers and aides were selected from among people who lived in the residential area being served.

Community service workers, also selected from the local neighborhoods, provided liaison with parents and community. They helped to carry out the health program, provided clothing where needed, obtained help with severe family problems and worked on the many difficulties that disrupt attendance by the children.

Altogether nearly 350 people from the school areas who had previously been without employment or working below their skills were employed by the Council. Directors of the project believed that persons who have lived under poverty conditions themselves can best teach others from the same background. "We were amazed at the number and qualifications of the people who responded to our first call for applicants," said Kim Jefferson, as he recalled the graduates from southern colleges, the Cuban refugees with teaching experience, and others variously qualified who came forward eagerly from the lowest income areas. Able teacher assistants and aides were also found among the mothers, with talents in languages, the arts, recreation and, most valuable of all, warm human relationships. The result was an intercultural staff widely varied economically, religiously and geographically.

27

Special Emphasis on Training. All the staff benefited from one full week of orientation sessions, in which they examined the special needs of children growing up in urban ghettos, the development of inter-personal relations, socio-economic views of the Newark community, the complex problems of the impoverished family and good nursery school procedures, values and curriculum. They next attended work-shop sessions with area boards and unit supervisors focused on special needs of the children and families in the particular neighborhood surrounding each Center.

By February each Center staff was functioning fully in its own area, and the intensive training took on "flesh" as they encountered squirming youngsters, questioning parents and the concrete assets (?) and liabilities of the community. Alternate Mondays were freed from classes so staff could concentrate on further training through a joint program of preschool education developed with neighboring Fairleigh Dickinson University. More than 100 staff members have also taken after-hours courses in early childhood education at Newark State College. A special training program was conducted for members of the Council of Jewish Women who volunteered as tutors in a high school equivalency program for staff members and parents who wanted this accreditation.

Parents Are Important, Too. Parents from the school areas were involved in the Pre-School Council from its first days and, through their small donations, supported the organization from February to September (1965) when the first federal grant came through. They began early to publicize the program in the neighborhoods, to recruit children and to serve on committees.

Teachers encouraged parents to participate in classroom activities. As they help with art programs, teach Spanish songs and go on trips with the children, the parents come to know each other, to understand better how the children learn and how parents can help at home. An "organized" parent program has discussed nutrition, fire hazards and planned parenthood along with air pollution, street cleaning, over-crowded schools, traffic safety and police protection.

A second request was submitted to OEO in April, 1966 and at the time of my visit to the project in June final action was still pending.[1]

---

[1] This second grant was not confirmed until November, 1966, though the Council received interim assurances that it would be approved. Since bills could not be paid by assurances, the forward thrust anticipated with the opening of classes in September was considerably slowed down. With the grant finally in hand, the program went into full swing again, starting with 92 classrooms.

28

Church Participation. From the beginning, Newark's religious leadership was active in initiating and influencing the direction of the city's total anti-poverty effort. On behalf of Protestants this action was carried by denominational leaders through the Greater Newark Council of Churches, where it was ably advanced by Kim Jefferson, council executive.

Members of churches located in areas of need, particularly parents of children enrollees, became front-line persuaders in getting church deacons, trustees and vestrymen to donate their buildings for classroom space, often including the further decision to pay the added costs of bringing their facilities up to sanitary and safety requirements.

Though very little was asked of churches outside the classroom areas, the Council of Churches did raise a small fund to pay some utility and custodial costs where the church with the space was unable to meet them. Council of Jewish Women volunteers provided tutorial service in the teacher-training program.

Altogether the contribution of the churches has been credited as a substantial factor in the success of Newark's Pre-School project.

HEAD START CHILD DEVELOPMENT CENTERS, CLEVELAND, OHIO

Mrs. E., speaking for all the mothers we'd like to thank you for all the wonderful things you've taught and shown our children. . . . You have done wonders with each one in the short time given you. . . . Our promise to you will be to continue your method of teaching and training our own, and to keep them just a little bit ahead. . . .

It is a good feeling for anyone to know "THEY BELONG" and you have given this feeling to our Children, we will not let them lose it. I for one, learned something from you, (that's a must). 1. To stop, listen and talk to our little ones. 2. To ask for their suggestions or ideas. 3. Not to compare. 4. Praise a little every now and then. . . . And always remember the world looks different to them and they are all different from anyone else (even Twins).

So thanks, thanks, again for your help with our children who are now "Ready for People."

(Signed) Mrs. S.[2]

[2] This letter was the spontaneous expression of appreciation written by the mother of a Head Start youngster at the Outhwaite Center to the head teacher, Mrs. Muriel Eichenbaum, at the end of the first Head Start series in 1965.

"We believe this letter describes the purpose, methods and results of a successful child development program," said Mrs. Robert A. Harvey, who from the beginning has chaired the important, very committed Head Start Administrative Committee of the Council of Churches of Greater Cleveland.

After watching youngsters, teachers and mother assistants in action at several Centers, I feel Mrs. S.'s letter reveals not only the methods and purpose of the program but the special qualities of warmth, understanding and emphasis on "the things that matter" that give the Cleveland Council of Churches' Head Start Project its high standing among all Head Start programs.

The Early Days. Soon after word came of the nationwide Head Start plan, child-concerned people and agencies of Cleveland held a ways and means discussion called by the local OEO agency. Here (on March 21, 1965), 5 agencies agreed to write separate proposals, allowing for diverse approaches but providing coordination of locations and needed overall services through the OEO office.

As one of these agencies, the Protestant Ministry to Poverty (joint arm of several major denominations in the Cleveland area) developed a proposal in cooperation with the Council of Churches. Written by Mrs. Paul Younger, wife of the director of PMP, this proposal was approved for sponsorship by the council at its executive board's April meeting, and the Head Start administrative committee was named.

During the next 2 months, a burst of cooperative action by many church groups and residents of areas to be served resulted in agreement on site locations for 16 Centers, contracting for hot meals (through the Board of Education) and medical services (through the Northeast Ohio Pediatric Society), selection of a director and hiring of head teachers, teaching assistants, custodial and office aides, and scheduling of a week-long training session for head teachers and parent workers at Western Reserve University.

On June 28, 16 Centers opened. Churches—usually piles of silent stone between Sundays—came alive with the sights and sounds of youngsters joyously preparing to become "ready for people." These first church-sponsored Centers, conducted for 8 weeks, involved 285 children, 75 teachers and parent counselors and 46 volunteers from the area.

Actually this summer program, known as Phase I, was only prologue in the Cleveland churches Head Start effort, with its major accomplishment being to foster Phase II—one of the first year-round Head Start projects.

30

Developing Phase II. Success with the summer program followed by extended "exploration with Washington, the local OEO office and others in the community" led to general agreement by mid-November that a proposal should be submitted by the Council of Churches to the local OEO board for a long-term Head Start project. Many meetings, proposals and months later this plan completed its tortuous journey through local, regional and national channels, and the Council of Churches' 1966-67 Head Start program was finally funded to provide classes for 390 children in 13 Centers for 44 weeks. These Centers opened on July 5, 1966, when the Catholic diocese also opened a similar program with 9 Centers and the Greater Cleveland Neighborhood Centers Association with 7.

Obviously this process required a vast amount of patient, understanding negotiation, political and nonpolitical, by many friends of Head Start throughout the city. The Council of Churches' Head Start administrative committee worked tirelessly and with great influence through it all. The special status of these independent programs enabled them to avoid much of the regimentation that has often discouraged other groups using public funds.

Under the year-round program, 2 class sessions are held daily from Tuesday through Friday with up to 15 children each. The staff spends Mondays in training, planning and record keeping. Each Center has a professionally trained head teacher and an assistant teacher. The latter, selected from the area served, gets on-the-job training through the Monday sessions and through courses available to all project workers through Western Reserve University. A medical coordinator provides comprehensive health services, one of the project's most valuable accomplishments.

Parents and Community. Experience throughout Phase I with the importance of parental influence resulted in addition of several new methods of enlisting parents in Phase II, starting with a parent counselor program under which a professionally trained counselor helps to develop parent involvement in 2 Centers with the help of one assistant (from the local area) in each. Forming a Center staff team with the 2 teachers, the counselor holds weekly parent meetings to discuss items of the parents' choice, such as child development, family budgets, nutrition and medical information. All programs aim to channel parents into daily contact with the Centers, where help is given with family problems or referral made to specialized counseling.

Two male program specialists from the area work with the fathers and men of the neighborhood to develop their participation in Center activities. Also older persons from the neighborhoods are selected as foster grandparents to work with broken homes or immature parents, trying to provide an image of what is involved in stable family life and how grandparents can help.

Parents, too, have helped to plan and make decisions regarding the total program from the earliest stages. Besides representation on the Head Start administrative committee, each Center has a Center committee including parents or others from the area, which carries policy-making responsibility for the Center and helps neighborhood and Center to understand and serve each other.

Church Involvement. Within the city's cooperative public-private framework, the Council of Churches of Christ of Greater Cleveland, acting through its Commission on Metropolitan Affairs under the direction of Rev. Charles W. Rawlings, became the sponsoring delegate agency for the churches' program. Developing the program obviously called for a large measure of local church member involvement, beginning with broad representation on the overall administrative committee. Here a close working relationship has developed between church leaders from the areas of greatest need, church specialists in nursery education and leaders from churches of advantaged areas of greater Cleveland, both city and suburb.

The administrative committee located the churches that opened their doors to the children for 8 centers in Phase I. "This was often the first real contact of the church with its surrounding community," said Mrs. Harvey. In Phase II the facilities of 11 churches, including Baptist, Disciples, Episcopal, Lutheran, Methodist, Presbyterian and United Church of Christ congregations, are being used.

In response to the Council of Churches' call for volunteer help, people from the Center neighborhoods and from city and suburban churches enlisted as classroom helpers; as sources of special skills in music, puppetry and other artistic engagements; as drivers of cars for trips to museums or zoos; as painters and renovators of buildings, playgrounds and equipment. Playtime supplies, wheel toys, climbing apparatuses came from many sources to brighten the eyes, strengthen the muscles and gladden the hearts of nearly 400 children.

Members of United Church Women through a "stitch in time" program provided 390 play kits, and a group of Jewish women through Hadassah provided health kits. Contributed dollars were used for training volunteers, tuition grants for nursery education courses, leasing a carryall bus and classroom and office needs.

Mrs. Harvey, summarizing local church involvement in the program, said, "Wherever we have pointed out the need, the churches have supplied it. It is most encouraging to find that a number of churches, not community-oriented before, are now becoming available."

PROJECT UPLIFT, PHOENIX, ARIZONA

An air of suppressed excitement was evident as Rev. Benjamin Brooks opened the door to a small room full of 3-year-olds. The center of interest was little Marie S., held proudly in the arms of Mrs. D., an assistant teacher in Project Uplift at Southminster Presbyterian Church in Phoenix, Arizona.

Marie had just thrilled them all by smiling faintly and reaching for a bright toy temptingly held out to her. "You see," Mrs. D. said, "this is the first time in the three weeks Marie's mother has been bringing her to us that she has shown even a flicker of response to anything that was said or offered to her."

Marie's mother is a widow, with 3 other children now in school. Her only support is from relief checks or what she can earn doing housework when someone will "mind" Marie. She came hesitatingly to the Center, afraid they "wouldn't be bothered with such a queer one," with whom her own efforts had made no progress. While Marie's was a stubborn case, I learned that her kind of withdrawal is not infrequent, particularly among the younger children of families where home care is minimal. Day care or preschool centers, where warm, understanding, individual attention is available, are often able to transform such a child gradually into a normally participating member of the group.

Southminster Presbyterian (USA) Church was established 12 years ago in a rapidly growing but economically, socially and racially mixed area of Phoenix. "Southminster is a neighborhood church with 180 members from the area," said Mr. Brooks, who has been its pastor throughout the period. Himself a Negro, Mr. Brooks has contributed the kind of "relevant" leadership that has helped to build the church into a racially and ethnically integrated and outward-looking fellowship, which demonstrates daily what can be meant by a "Christian presence" in the neighborhood.

Two-Pronged Approach to Children and Parents. "Our experience convinced us," explained Mr. Brooks, "that an approach that focuses only upon the child is a necessary, but not sufficient, condition to achieve positive results. Hence Project Uplift utilizes a two-pronged approach to the children and to their parents simultaneously." The two-way program consists of 1) preschool education and training, with custodial care, for children of working mothers or mothers attending classes preparatory to gainful employment, and 2) a program of counseling and training for the parents.

This program, presented as a community action project (not Head Start), was funded in October 1965, for one year for $105,907, with Southminster Church as the direct contracting agency. The church's "in kind" contribution included the use (for 5 days a week) of its entire educational facilities, estimated at $12,800.

The program at Southminster, emphasizing young children and parents, grew out of a teen-age tutoring project. As one of the church's first outreach efforts, the tutoring program immediately caught on and still functions through the help of volunteers. "Our reading of the signs of the times among these teen-agers led us to conclude that with them we were beginning too late. What children in this neighborhood need is a developmental program in their earliest formative years, and this is what we are seeking to provide in Project Uplift," said Dr. Morrison Warren, child education specialist and member of its Professional Advisory Committee.

The 100 children enrolled at Southminster include 3-, 4- and 5-year-olds (since the public schools provide no kindergarten classes in the area). To accommodate working mothers the Center is open from 7 A.M. until 6 P.M. Besides Mr. Brooks, who serves as project director, and one supervising teacher, the full-time teaching staff includes 3 group teachers (with professional training) and 4 teacher aides. Four substitute teachers and teacher aides are also employed part-time, as are music, arts, crafts and drama teachers. Psychological, educational and social work consultants are paid fees for their services as needed. A head cook and 2 helpers serve the children a hot meal at noon and 2 light snacks during the day.

All employees are from the project area, except for some professionals not locally available. Instructors from the College of Education at Arizona State University provide in-service training, and health services are available through the Maricopa Health Department.

While Project Uplift's primary goal is to create a new generation of healthy and productive citizens, its secondary goal is to help rehabilitate the parents of these children "right here and now." Willingness of the parents to take part in the parent education, while not an absolute requirement, is one basis for selecting children for the school, in order that both thrusts reach the same families.

The threefold aim of the children's program—overcoming handicaps of the language-starved home through development of language facility, extending the variety of prelearning experiences and strengthening the culturing process—applies similarly to the parents' program. To it is added emphasis on understanding the need for education and for child training. The process is mostly clinical group counseling with experienced psychologists. Three group sessions are held weekly, with each parent attending one session of at least 90 minutes, and opportunity is provided for individual sessions with the therapists.

Extent of Church Involvement. "As you can see," said Benjamin Brooks, "this kind of activity carried on and supported by a single church—a small and far from affluent one at that—calls forth a high degree of commitment of both time and money from its membership." He estimated that at least 50 percent of the members either take part in a program or help in other volunteer ways.

Upon endorsement of the project by the Presbyterian Synod of Arizona, the Southminster board of directors entered directly into contractual relations with the government. They are also responsible for general oversight of the church's total outreach activity, assisted by a volunteer professional advisory board, which helped to develop the project and is deeply committed to its success.

Project Uplift is a striking example of what can be done by a single congregation when it identifies wholeheartedly with its surrounding community, and draws upon the people of the whole community for help as well as participation in the program's benefits. Favored with a neighborhood of mixed races, economic strata and leadership potential, Southminster has made wide use of these personnel resources.

Mr. Brooks believes that the churches, with their wide experience in meeting people's needs and the wealth of knowledge and ability in their members, should take the lead in attempts to eliminate poverty. Southminster has committed itself wholly and most effectively to helping point the way.

THE CHILD DEVELOPMENT GROUP OF MISSISSIPPI

In the summer of 1965 some 1,200 residents (mostly Negroes) of 20 of the poorest counties of Mississippi accomplished a modern miracle.

With funds from OEO and a small central staff, parents from the cotton fields and small hamlets of the Delta area—constituting the Child Development Group of Mississippi—located, repaired, staffed, equipped and operated 84 preschool centers. These centers provided 7 weeks of unprecedented educational opportunity for 6,000 of the state's most disadvantaged 4-, 5- and 6-year-old children.

When the first OEO funding expired in late August 1965, several Centers continued on a volunteer basis. As the second grant was further delayed, more and more parents rallied to continue the programs

35

with volunteer help and contributions, with the result that 49 of the original 84 centers continued and several new ones came into being. "These Centers functioned from early fall 1965 until late February 1966 without one dollar of financial aid from anywhere outside of the center communities," explained John Mudd, director of CDGM.

In February, 1966, OEO signed the second grant, giving the CDGM program $5.6 million for 124 centers in 28 counties to run through August, 1966. When I visited them in July, 12,145 children were busily "developing" in 121 centers.

Obviously a social movement of this magnitude, with its unique involvement of the normally uninvolved Negro population, did not happen without stirring up political resistance. This resistance began to develop in Mississippi almost with the opening of the first Center. Some crosses and even some Centers were burned; threats of dispossession, job loss and physical violence were made and frequently carried out. Failure to halt this "threatening advance of the illiterate poor" at the state level was followed by protests from Mississippi congressional leaders to the source of the "trouble" in Washington.

During the summer of 1966, the full force of this disapproval was directed against further funding. This generated counter pressure from influential "nonpolitical" friends of the project, by this time nationally endorsed by educational, religious and social organizations. At the present time, the political forces appear to be winning, for OEO has officially turned down the third request. Since the defenders are not giving up easily, however, some measure of public funding may still be approved.[3]

How CDGM Came to Be. Whether or not this potent organization continues in its present form, it is essential that the story of its origin, development and reliance on religious forces be included here.

Negro leaders of the Delta area who had been active in the civil rights movement wanted to see anti-poverty programs started in their neighborhoods, and they had a powerful ally in the nationally sponsored and operated Delta Ministry. Even before the development of OEO's program, a small group had discussed the prospects for setting up 2 or 3 pilot child development centers. "The response to this suggestion was overwhelming," said John Mudd, "and the Delta Ministry helped greatly both then and throughout our organizing period."

Bringing this development into focus with OEO's Head Start plans as they emerged, this group decided to form the Child Development

[3] CDGM has subsequently been given a third grant of $8 million for 1967.

Group of Mississippi "to develop and operate a summer program for 4,500 preschool children across the State." A widely representative board of directors was organized, a small staff selected, an OEO request developed and an intensive campaign started to enlist parents in planning and organizing the local Centers. The Board of Mary Holmes Junior College (supported by the Presbyterian (USA) Board of National Missions) agreed to serve as grantee and present the request to OEO.

Forming and Operating the Centers. Each community desiring a child development center selects a representative group of parents and others to form a Center committee, which must 1) find an adequate location (often an abandoned one-room school or church, or weekday use of facilities in a functioning church), 2) put it in shape to meet minimum sanitary and safety standards and 3) show sufficient parental support to enroll at least 15 children per class unit.

The Center committee is responsible for operating the Center and enlisting help in remodeling, repairing, equipping and maintaining the facilities. The committee has the final decision in hiring and firing employees and planning transportation, meals and health services. It is estimated that more than 1,000 local residents have served on these committees and another 1,000 to 2,000 neighborhood volunteers have helped with facilities, equipment, health, recreation and entertainment.

Each center is staffed with one professional person with special skills in child development and community action, plus staff trainees and aides, with priority given to persons from the neighborhoods qualified through experience, interest and/or "natural ability with children and people."

Each of 15 area staffs includes one administrator, one area teacher guide and 2 organizers, also selected from the area. During the summer of 1965, the area staff helpers were college students from inside and outside the state. Each was assisted by local coordinators "who learned enough during the summer to take the place of the students when they left in the fall," explained Mrs. Polly Greenberg, director of teacher training activities. Continuous, intensive training opportunities were provided for the Project's total staff of 2,150 parent or community-based employees.

Visits to Two Centers. When I visited the CDGM in July, Mrs. Greenberg took me to some of the nearest Centers. As we approached the Center at Bolton, she warned that we might find it badly disrupted,

37

HOW CHURCHES FIGHT POVERTY

since 2 days earlier the old school building, which the Center committee had finished renovating and equipping less than a month before, had burned to the ground.

To our surprise we were greeted, as we drew up beside the burned-out structure, by the smiling head teacher, Mr. H., a retired former principal in the old school. We soon learned the cause of his smile. "We are now convinced after studying conditions of the building and hearing from persons who arrived as soon as the fire was discovered," he explained, "that the fire was caused by a defective gas heater and not set by unfriendly folk, as we feared." (In support of the fears, I learned that at least 2 other Centers had been burned in the past month, clearly by nonfriends of the project.)

Since it was a warm July day, "school" was going forward with a lively singing game under the shade of nearby trees. Half of the group had been taken to a neighboring public school (quickly offered by a local school board),[4] where the daily hot meal had been prepared in the modern kitchen of this newer (but still "separate but equal") school building. There seemed to be only one as yet unsolved problem —a quiet space for the really young ones to have their rest time. "This makes it especially difficult for some of the children," a young mother aide explained, "since they must start soon on their long journey home and some come from 50 miles away."

At True Light Center in Anguilla, "a far piece" down the hot highway, we found six 3-year-olds sleeping soundly on the bare floor of a small, one-room church building in which the Sunday benches had been pushed back against the walls. Under the watchful eye of a teacher aide these youngsters napped peacefully, quite undisturbed by the noisy excitement of the older group just outside.

In spite of limited quarters and other difficulties the children at True Light Center were being taught, played with, read to, carefully watched over and cherished, many of them for the first time in their meager, love-starved lives. They were responding with a bright-eyed, friendly, boisterous eagerness which, to my thinking, added up, in this one otherwise barren, hopeless spot, to reward enough for the cost of the whole nationally supported project.

How Has the Church Been Involved?   The Child Development Group of Mississippi is one of the few *local* anti-poverty programs in which the National Council of Churches has had some part. Until it

---

[4] I learned that the Bolton Center was one of the few that had benefited from the beginning from the sympathetic support of the whole community, both white and Negro.

became active in the issue of the third OEO grant, this involvement was only indirect through the Delta Ministry. Nationally, the Board of National Missions of the Presbyterian Church USA has also been concerned through sponsorship of the CDGM OEO grants by its Mary Holmes Junior College.

The Delta Ministry and the religious forces with which it worked within the state are credited with making possible the project's early development. This account and reports from the Centers frequently refer to active relationships with local churches. These are almost all Negro churches. "They were among the few going institutions in the neighborhoods which could be counted on for leadership," said John Mudd.

When the controversy broke out in Washington over the 1967 grant, national Protestant church bodies were joined in CDGM's defense by Roman Catholic and Jewish groups. Many other civic, educational and welfare groups added their voices in protest against the threatened cut-off of funds.

The whole experience of CDGM graphically disproves the stereotype of "poor people" as basically inept and helpless, which is held by many not familiar with the "culture of poverty." What seems to go unrecognized is the power of two potent, but rare, things in poverty-land—*opportunity* and *hope*—to bring into action the native ability and dogged determination that "poor people" possess in equal measure with all men.

Considering the many rural areas of the country in which a large-scale program such as this could bring similar opportunity and hope to many of today's small-farm and small-hamlet poor people, CDGM's challenge to the churches, especially state councils of churches, is unmistakable.

If they were counted, I am sure the number of churches that have involved themselves in preschool programs serving disadvantaged children would total in the thousands. In some cases single congregations have organized and conducted either preschool or the fuller day-care programs. Frequently 2 or more churches have united to provide a neighborhood service. Many child care programs are also components of larger, more inclusive programs conducted by community centers.

Programs directed to the care and education of disadvantaged children differ at many points, depending on varying needs, varying philosophies of approach and education, varying degrees of intensity, commitment and financial support. The extent and kind of church involvement also differs considerably from project to project.

It is possible, however, to identify at least 5 characteristics or trends common to most programs.

First is the mutual concern to expand educational horizons and opportunities for the nation's 3-, 4- and 5-year-olds whose home environments fail so dismally.

Second is the emphasis on spontaneous, creative and developmental activity, summed up by one teacher who said: "We want this to be a *play* school, not a lesson school."

Third is a striving for a workable balance between professional training in child care and education and parental experience in child-rearing in deprivation and poverty. An unexpected bonus of the whole anti-poverty program has been "a new and more objective understanding of poor children" by both educators and parents.

Fourth is the effort to enlist as large a proportion of project committees, staff and volunteers as possible from residents of the areas being served. The extent to which the projects have been staffed by unemployed, underemployed or often first-time employed persons from the poverty areas has been phenomenal.

Finally, the most evident and increasing emphasis in every program is on enlistment and education of parents. The eagerness with which most parents respond was expressed by one who said: "This is my chance to get sort of a Head Start too and it has really helped me."

3 Education and Education Aids

"Give a man a fish, he'll eat for a day; teach him to fish, he'll feed himself."

This old Gaelic proverb expresses the working philosophy of the Voluntary Improvement Program (VIP) of St. Bridget's Church in St. Louis. It might well be adopted as the working principle of the large segment of anti-poverty workers who consider education to be the bedrock stepping stone out of poverty.

In the United States 60 million adults lack a high school diploma. Of these, 8.3 million have had less than 5 years of schooling. These figures explain why the need for education—most often basic education, beginning with the three R's—has loomed up before practically every group seeking to help lift the burdens of low income people in city, suburb or rural community. The figures explain why impoverished adults, when given a choice, most often say: "Somewhere we missed out; now we want to learn how to live and work in today's world. Teach us to read, write, and figure."

The specter of adding to the 60 million via the "dropout" doorway helps to account for the hours of tutoring and being tutored at grade and high school levels which is another large sector on the poverty battlefront.

Like children and families, education too has always been a primary concern of the churches. Not surprising, therefore, is the extent to which religious forces have taken the lead in many communities to help people in poverty in their quest for educational opportunities, ranging from preschool through adult years. An educational "component" is provided as one, often predominant, feature of almost every anti-poverty project. Some projects concentrate wholly on education, usually directed to the learning needs of a particular age group. This chapter describes programs for adults, grade school children and youth.

EDUCATION FOR ADULTS

LITERACY VOLUNTEERS OF SYRACUSE, NEW YORK

"Free! to adults—Learn to Read" says the flier directed to prospective students by the renowned Literacy Volunteers of Syracuse. "Though adults who can't read live in a blurred world," says Mrs. Robert J. Colvin, originator, promoter and "mainstay" of the Syracuse project, "they do have normal eyesight, and many have learned to recognize the word 'free.' They take our flier when they see this and then get someone to explain what else it says."

What else the flier says has been the best news of their lives for the thousands of men and women in the Syracuse area and, through the idea's spread, in many other communities of New York and other states, who have been taught to read and write by more than 1,000 deeply committed Literacy Volunteers since the project started in February, 1963.

This productive enterprise began when Mrs. Colvin, imaginative and energetic housewife, civic leader, and former business woman, became intrigued with a series of articles in a Syracuse newspaper about the millions of functional illiterates (persons over 25 with less than 5 years of schooling) who still live in this nation with the world's most highly rated educational system. Some follow-up showed that, according to the 1960 Census, 800,000 of these illiterates live in New York state (the largest number of any state), with more than 11,000 in her own Onondaga County.

Mrs. Colvin then set in motion a chain of activities (including a round of Laubach-method training for herself) which resulted in organization of the Literacy Volunteers of Syracuse under the sponsorship of the Syracuse United Church Women.

One of the first things Mrs. Colvin and her group of enthusiastic, but largely uninformed, helpers had to learn was the special hiddenness of illiteracy. As one describer has summed it up: "The usual symptom of this unusual disease is elaborate fakery; if someone hands you a paper you nod knowingly, smile if the other man smiles and hand it back. Or you say you left your glasses at home. The illiterate's greatest fears are laughter and the word 'stupid' . . . so he tries to hide his problem. Often whole families are co-conspirators; they hide together."[1]

[1] Richard G. Case, "The Wonderful World of C-A-T," *Syracuse Herald-American*, February 27, 1966.

On the other hand, adults often seek help because they don't want their children to learn about their lack of education or they want to be able to help with homework. Actually the realities of trying to find or keep a job in today's "educated" working world produce most of the applicants. The Syracuse program provides that the training shall be confidential, using the one pupil–one teacher method to assure that "no one but you and your teacher will be involved in your training."

Teachers meet their students for one hour twice a week at a mutually convenient time and place. Places with a quiet workroom are located in churches, social agencies and libraries. Teachers, including businessmen, doctors, lawyers, editors, secretaries, retired teachers, as well as "freer-time" housewives (every kind of person who cares), are recruited throughout the area. The teachers are trained in 10-hour workshops, held at frequent intervals to take care of new recruits. The training is free, but each teacher pays $5 for her materials. Each teacher reports regularly on the progress of his or her student and may request help, if needed, from a teacher-consultant.

The pupil-to-pupil "grapevine" is the best source for student enrollment. Press, radio and TV announcements also back up the thousands of fliers distributed through welfare and employment offices, social agencies, health departments, NAACP and storefront churches. Those who enroll range from teen-agers to 70-year-olds, from housewives to preachers.

When I followed Mrs. Colvin on her busy rounds one day last summer (1966), she brought out from her well-ordered (home-basement) office one of her newest pictures. The setting was a local supermarket; the persons of interest, Mrs. Colvin and her latest pupil, Mr. S. Sitting on a customers' bench at the front of the store, surrounded by empty boxes and cash registers, they were engaged in their twice-weekly study hour. "Mr. S. and I have been working together for 2 years," said Mrs. Colvin. "He is from Florida, and had to really start from the very bottom. While serving as a preacher at one of the smaller churches, he has worked at night as a dishwasher to eke out his income. He has recently taken a daytime job at the Shopping Center, so we meet at 8 A.M. at the Acme Market for study before he goes to work." Mrs. Colvin said the store manager gladly agreed to let them use the customer sitting space while the store was being readied for opening at 9 A.M. "Because he's so busy with a full-time job as well as his church responsibilities, Mr. S. can't give as much time to studies as he wants—but he never gives up and is determined to get his diploma. I'm very proud of his accomplishments."

The literacy program trains adults through the fourth grade only.

43

Upon completing grade 4 reading level each student receives a diploma and is then encouraged, as many do, to go into the public school adult program.

The program's success with adults led the Syracuse Board of Education to request the help of Literacy Volunteers with the schools' teen-age "nonreaders." When I was in Syracuse, Mrs. Colvin had already assigned 17 teachers to various city schools.

With these achievements, it was inevitable that Literacy Volunteers should spread far beyond its starting place. In 1965 the United Church Women of New York State endorsed the program and promoted its extension statewide through state Literacy Leaders Training Workshops. Watching a training-workshop film, prepared for the program by Syracuse's station WHEN-TV, leaders are shown how to start a similar program in any area: how to teach basic English; contact volunteer teachers; locate students; find places for teaching; set up a new readers' library; and keep records on students' progress. Fifty-seven workshops have trained more than 1,000 teachers, and programs are underway in 20 communities. Workshop registrants are also accepted from other states, looking toward the program's still wider spread and usefulness.

Where do the churches come in? In Literacy Volunteers it is church people, rather than the churches as such, that have been involved. The whole undertaking has depended to a great extent on the extraordinary drive, organizing ability and sheer "stick-to-itiveness" of Ruth Colvin. As her idea took on form and substance, so did the need for some organized base. Aware of the interest of United Church Women in the welfare of underprivileged people, Mrs. Colvin turned to them and received the backing needed to give it standing as a community-endorsed enterprise.

Approval by United Church Women made the program more visible to women's groups in the local churches. More teacher volunteers, both women *and their husbands*, were acquired as a result. Small contributions were also realized.

In fact, the program's financing (more notably the lack of it) is another awe-inspiring feature of Literacy Volunteers. I smiled as I read in the account of one observer that, "the church women's Syracuse Plan costs nothing. It uses nonprofessional volunteer teachers." It does cost its beneficiaries nothing except their time, and the same may be true in a sense of the teachers (except for the $5 "materials" fee). Space, otherwise unused, is provided free by churches and other local groups. Office space, supplies, equipment, stenographic and mimeo services, planning, organization, curriculum development, teacher recruitment and training, student recruitment, public relations and files (already full of teacher and student records) have also been contributed *free* by Mrs. Colvin and a small supporting committee.

Up to the time of my visit (July 1966) the project income from the beginning (excluding the teachers' fees) had probably totalled less than $1,000, contributed mainly by individual friends. An appeal letter from United Church Women to the churches produced several amounts of $5 and $10. Mrs. Colvin's own church gave $100. A big boon came through the production "for free" of the workshop film by WHEN-TV.

In truth it can be said, "never has so much been accomplished with so little" (surely not in the annals of anti-poverty warfare).[2]

VOLUNTARY IMPROVEMENT PROGRAM, ST. LOUIS, MISSOURI

Teaching men (and women) to fish, as well as many other things, is the daily (including Sunday) concern of the staff and small army of volunteers of the Voluntary Improvement Program (VIP) of St. Bridget's Roman Catholic Parish in the center of a once-fashionable, but now rapidly deteriorating, area of St. Louis.

St. Bridget's Church was built in 1860. As the original residents of the area prospered and moved out, waves of new immigrants moved in, the latest being Negroes from the South. Some years ago when buildings were being demolished to make way for the vast Pruitt-Igoe public housing project, the Archdiocese considered tearing the church down. It was a good day for the new residents of the area (now scarcely any Irish and less than 1,000 Catholics) when its owners decided instead to repair the historic church and build a new rectory and school to serve the community.

Under the leadership of its far-sighted pastor, Father John A. Shocklee, a multi-faceted program—described by one observer as "Father Shocklee's guerrilla war on poverty"—now brings help and hope to the 29,000 low-income residents of the area.

Most outreaching of St. Bridget's many "arms" is VIP, the basic education program for men, women, and older youths which began in 1962, when visits to every one of the 2,800 families in Pruitt-Igoe revealed the nearly unanimous desire of the people for opportunity to

[2] As I write this (February 1967), Mrs. Colvin tells me she has since had a foundation contribution of $1,500. Also, on advice of friendly lawyers (contributed), the "committee" is now in process of incorporating, making the project into an official nonprofit organization, with contributions to it tax deductible. All concerned seem hopeful that this will result in a substantial rise in contributions.

45

continue their education. VIP's adult tutoring program is St. Bridget's answer to that need. Its objective is to provide education at whatever level is needed to equip its participants to qualify for the State High School Equivalency Diploma.

Enrollment in VIP has grown from 42 to 460 in its first 2 years, and more than 100 applicants crowd its waiting list. Students and teachers come together for 2 hours on Sunday afternoons and Tuesday and Thursday evenings, and a special Neighborhood Youth Corps group of high school dropouts meets Wednesday nights. Each teacher tutors 2 students at a time.

Applicants take informal placement tests to determine their starting levels, then go on the waiting list for an opening at that level. Once accepted for training, each student is assigned to a group including a reading teacher, a math teacher, and 3 other students at the same level. He or she remains in this group until taking the H.S.E. tests. Much of the program's very high rating comes from the fact that almost 95 percent of VIP students taking H.S.E. tests received diplomas.

All teachers are volunteers, coming from religious groups, public and parochial schools and the city's many colleges and universities. Teachers attend a monthly in-service training program which stresses understanding the inner city environment of the students and the special needs of adult learners. A master teacher (experienced and professional) is available for help as needed for every 5 to 7 groups.

During its early stages VIP was supported entirely by funds from St. Bridget's Church "and generous friends." An OEO grant has helped with expansion, though it still provides less than $7 per student per year, plus the salary of a full-time administrative assistant to Father Shocklee. Additional funds are being sought from private sources to provide teacher transportation, more study materials, audio-visual equipment and better staff training programs.

St. Bridget's is also serving its needy community through several low-cost housing construction and rehabilitation projects, a growing credit union, a job counseling and placement service, a big brother–big sister program, a weekly Citizen's Training Seminar (CITRAS) and encouragement of community organization through block units affiliated with the Urban League of St. Louis.

"Those who work at St. Bridget's use every resource they know or can learn about," said Sister Frances Cabrini. As an impressed *Post-Dispatch* reporter summed up: "Father Shocklee is the catalyst in a series of human improvement programs—all of them bringing together middle-class people who want to help and poorer people who want to better themselves." Both seem to be profiting from the encounter.

46

CITY-BOUND MIGRANTS FROM APPALACHIA

Among the toughest "fronts" of the poverty war are the attempts being made to enlarge the educational, social and cultural opportunities of the proud, but often very impoverished, families who leave their homes on the unproductive mountainsides of Appalachia for the unknown, usually unfriendly, streets of the inner city metropolis. One significant approach is being made through Grace House in Richmond, Virginia.

GRACE HOUSE IN RICHMOND, VIRGINIA

Grace House, started in 1963 as a nursery school project by a group of women from St. James' Episcopal Church, is located in a compact area of the inner city to which come most often the in-migrants from Appalachian mountain areas. Many are crowded into two-room "apartments" in buildings where in some cases as many as 20 to 25 people have to share one bathroom. Rents are high and so is transiency.

The value of the project not only to the children but to the whole area led six other congregations—Lutheran, Presbyterian, Methodist, United Church of Christ, Roman Catholic and Jewish—to join in sponsoring it.

Although the child development program still remains paramount, its sponsors soon realized the importance of work with the parents in efforts to improve home conditions and attitudes. At this point the program expanded to become a small, but strategically important, neighborhood center. Mrs. Arthur Spangenthal, a Quaker from Pennsylvania who is professionally trained in early childhood education, was joined, as director, by 2 trained assistants.

Though enlisting them has proved difficult, mothers have been gradually brought into the Center through a weekly "coffee hour," and have enrolled in serving, cooking and basic education classes. A once-a-week "clothes day" during which mothers select needed shoes, dresses and other items for the family is also welcomed, and where possible small amounts are paid for the articles selected.

"One of the greatest problems," said Mrs. Spangenthal, "is in establishing communication, either between the families themselves, who share little, if any, feeling of neighborliness with each other, or between the families and the Center." With few goals and only limited desire for personal improvement, many coming to the area seem to live for the moment, with little or no planning for the future. High

47

mobility is a further complicating factor in maintaining the Center's activities.

Step by step, however, the patient, understanding, often ingenious efforts of the small but able staff are penetrating the walls of fear and withdrawal with which many of the mountain people surround themselves. A tribute to their effectiveness is included in a recent report on the Grace House program by a Community Council Evaluation Committee: "Grace House is meeting a pressing community need in an effective and dynamic way."

Grace House, like many others, is making judicious use of volunteers. With them, as with the staff, a whole "other way" of doing things has to be learned before helpful interaction with the families becomes possible.

TUTORIAL AND STUDY-HELP PROGRAMS FOR CHILDREN AND YOUTH

Early in the 1960's we belatedly discovered the alarming rate of school "dropouts" and the lifetime handicap lack of schooling imposes on many youths, particularly those from impoverished neighborhoods. This discovery led to a wide variety of youth-help programs, among the most effective being the one teacher–one pupil tutorial and remedial reading projects.

As the tutorial experimenters gained experience with the slow learners and with the personal, family and environmental causes of their difficulties, attention turned also to preventive programs with potential dropouts. These programs frequently begin with children who show poor reading or learning tendencies in the earliest grades. Another soon-revealed need was for quiet, supervised study rooms where youngsters from distracting home situations could have periods of uninterrupted "homework."

Churches, church groups or agencies, with virtually untapped volunteer teacher resources and large amounts of unused space, were among the first to initiate and then to expand tutorial, remedial reading and quiet study programs.

ST. JOHN'S WORKSHOP, BOSTON, MASSACHUSETTS

St. John's Episcopal Church, in the Roxbury Crossing community of Boston, conducts a Community Information Center and tutorial program in an adjacent, church-owned building known as The Workshop. The tutoring program is for children from the first through the sixth grades. The community around the Center has a population of about 9,000, with 7,000 living in 3 public housing developments. Well over half of the public housing families receive some form of public assistance.

The tutoring program started some years ago when Charles Glenn, then the rector at St. John's, saw a desperate need among children for development of the elemental skills of reading and writing. He organized a volunteer tutorial program of basic reading for the first three grades.

This program now reaches 95 to 100 children from all sections of the community with remedial work in language arts (reading, writing and speaking) and math. Each child comes for an hour and a half twice a week. Teachers work with the children in 14 classes of not more than 4 pupils per teacher. One professional teacher is employed for half-time from a small OEO grant. In addition, 21 local mothers and high school girls are hired as teachers, and there are 15 student volunteers from Wellesley College. Reading teachers receive 18 hours of training by Mrs. Glenn, director of the tutorial program. Twelve to 18 hours of training have also been given to 4 high school students and 4 local mothers who teach the mathematics classes. Teachers are given further preparation through in-service training and a staff meeting each week.

A core of the St. John's program is this training of local women to teach the needed skills. To date about 40 mothers and 15 high school girls have been related to the program, and many have gone on to other full-time teaching jobs. "An exciting development," says Charles Glenn, "is that the Welfare Department has begun to pay salaries—$15 a week for 10 hours—to the teachers who are on ADC (Aid to Dependent Children), under the Work Experience Program. They are also referring women on ADC who want jobs to St. John's for training."

The large Community Information Center also housed in the Workshop offers general information, job referral and community organization activities, aimed at "increasing the knowledge and effectiveness of low income people in dealing with all aspects of the 'system' and toward developing a more independent and self-sufficient community." The Center activities are supported mainly by church and other contributed funds, Mrs. Miriam Becton, its director, told me. The Center was also anticipating the help of a corps of VISTA volunteers beginning in the fall of 1966.

CHRISTIAN SERVICE CENTER, INC., SOUTH BEND, INDIANA

How one thing leads to another when a good thing once gets started is illustrated by the experience of the Evangelical United Brethren,

Methodist and Church of the Brethren denominations in South Bend, Indiana, in jointly organizing the Christian Service Center, Inc.

Surveying the "frightening list of needs" confronting the community, the group felt that one of the most crucial was what to do about "the consistent under-achievement of children and youth in their school performance." Five programs were set up to provide some remedies. These included a school-readiness nursery (for deprived children during the year before they entered kindergarten), a corrective reading program (for school-age children with obvious deficiencies, referred from public school classes), community study halls ("a warm, quiet place" with reference materials and teachers available), weekday religious education (for children from first through sixth grades) and a 7-days-on-a-farm summer camp program.

The work did not end there, though. The nursery program led to a summer preschool program and a Mothers' Club agenda, offering "real therapy sessions for the mothers" and (with the help of lay volunteers) "some significant relationships across cultural and racial lines." The study hall emerged into an extensive tutoring program (with university student tutors) and a spontaneous youth discussion group, "Sound Off," in which white and Negro groups engage in productive dialogue.

Youth interest groups, field trips, women's sewing classes, adult literacy classes and a college incentive program joined the swelling list of activities. The project staff includes one coordinator, 6 full-time volunteers from the Brethren Volunteer Service and up to 60 volunteer workers from South Bend churches "giving a minimum of one-half day a week." One unexpected result of the project was "the changed lives of the volunteers who became involved in mission."

VOLUNTEER TUTORING PROGRAM, CHICAGO, ILLINOIS

The Mayor's Committee on New Residents (arm of the Chicago Commission on Human Relations) lists, coordinates and serves a large group of tutoring projects, which have spread to almost every corner of Chicago.

The Summer 1966 Directory includes 107 programs reaching all ages from preschoolers to adults. Thirty-six are sponsored and housed by local church congregations, synagogues, schools or area ministries. While the projects continued to provide tutoring in reading and mathematics, the 1966 emphasis was on cultural enrichment programs in music, art appreciation and a wide variety of field trips.

Recognizing the services contributed from the many churches and synagogues, from high schools, sororities, etc., the Mayor's Commit-

tee gives greatest credit for the rapid expansion of the tutoring programs to the college students. "Started by Northwestern University
and University of Chicago Student organizations, we wonder if they
fully realize the magnificent gift of their time."

The unspectacular but cumulative success of the thousands of tutoring programs organized so widely in the last 2 or 3 years moved
an editorial commentator in the *Saturday Review* to accord them a
very high place in today's "educational revolution," emerging mainly
from the War on Poverty. "Tutoring disadvantaged children is a little
like being a scoutmaster or a hospital volunteer: It seems to do no
harm and may even do some good. . . . Now it is becoming apparent
that the tutors are neither harmless nor ineffective. They may, in fact,
constitute the most powerful force for educational reform on the
American scene."[3]

Citing a "thorough and well-written survey" prepared for the OEO,
he notes that what had been thought to be a series of scattered little
tutoring programs actually involves some 200,000 tutors working with
approximately a million children. These programs, "operating with
budgets that would paralyze any self-respecting, professional grant
administrator," are demonstrating the possibility of self-help and the
viability of "using amateurs to cope with the failures that the professionals leave behind."

In addition to the kinds of education-centered programs here described, education, "from the cradle to the grave" and of many varie-
ties, is a direct or indirect purpose of many other anti-poverty programs.

From these educational activities at least 3 important factors emerge.
First are the great variety of approaches and types of sponsorship used
by religious groups in educational involvement of disadvantaged children, youth and adults. Though the programs described have been
sponsored by United Church Women, by church community centers
and by one or several denominational bodies, many educational programs, especially tutoring, are initiated and operated by single church
congregations or jointly by 2 or more congregations.

Second is the unprecedented extent to which volunteers have proved
both willing and able to provide the person-to-person guidance that is
a core requirement of these programs. Trained by professionals and
provided in most cases with professional help "on call," thousands of
church-connected students (high school and college) and adults have

[3] Peter Schrag, "Voices in the Classroom." *Saturday Review*, Feb. 18,
1967, p. 92.

given—and gained—invaluable help from their contribution of time, knowledge, understanding and energy. This contribution is what has held out-of-pocket costs to a bare minimum, and is a compelling reason why they can and should be sponsored even more widely by church groups and congregations.

Third is the recognition these programs invariably provide of the need to root out other root causes (besides inadequate education) that continue to keep poor and make miserable the lives of residents of ghetto areas, urban and rural, across the country.

Obviously meeting problems like these is a big part of what the whole war against poverty is about. Education can and must help to remove the "poverty of personality" that handicaps nearly every impoverished person. This will not be accomplished permanently, however, as long as the individual's life must be lived from day to day under the other galling realities of slum-ridden America.

4 Family Renewal Through Housing and Services

To keep a family intact today there is no greater material need than a decent, adequate dwelling place. If that dwelling is on a clean street in a congenial neighborhood, the chances of the family's holding together are even greater. Almost beyond belief, however, to millions of well-housed Americans, is the frustration confronting the many low-income families forced to move out of the place, however dilapidated or inadequate, they have managed to call "home."

Acres of "concrete cities" with their thousands of low-cost housing units are being provided by public housing projects in practically every growing city. Yet the bulldozers of urban renewal and the ravages of decay still displace poor families faster than new living places are created for them.

Family welfare, too, has long been a major concern of the churches. Starting with the families "of the faithful," it has carried over in many ways to families in general and particularly to the "needy." In recent years, however, the problems of families in need and the requirements for help have become so vast that they have far outrun the resources of churches and other private groups for meeting them. In spite of continuing private interest (such as family service societies, child adoption agencies), the bulk of family welfare responsibility has had to be assumed by public agencies and supported by public funds.

For a time this seemed to be the answer. By a kind of evolving mutual consent the public agencies took over care of the "needy" families, while the private (including the church) groups concentrated on the growing psychological and social problems of their member, or kin, families. Today the situation of families in need has retrogressed, however, to the point where the tragic inadequacy of the impersonal, assembly-line process of public welfare agencies has become so evident that private groups can no longer ignore it.

With understandable enthusiasm a growing number of congregations, councils of churches and more recently denominational bodies have entered or are about to enter upon home-building projects. These projects are of varying sizes and involve a wide variety of private-public financing arrangements. Many have been designed to provide comfortable, modern (not necessarily low-cost) living arrangements for old people. Yet most of these projects serve middle or upper income families, not families living in poverty.

In addition, it takes time to plan, finance and build large-scale housing. The need of poor families is desperate *now*. Attempts at family survival under subsistence living today have become so complicated that even trying to help seems difficult. Fortunately, however, there are courageous, informed and not easily discouraged people, many church-related, who are seeking to meet just this kind of need, in the "here and now." Accounts of some of these pioneering family-service groups are the subject of this chapter.

HOPE, INC., CLEVELAND, OHIO

Rev. Walter Grevatt, pastor of the Hough Avenue United Church of Christ, and Father Albert Koklowsky, pastor of Our Lady of Fatima Catholic Church, have taken the lead in organizing a unique housing and human renewal project in Cleveland's troubled Hough area. The association, called HOPE, Inc. (Housing Our People Economically), was formed in June 1965, as a nonprofit organization.

On HOPE's board of trustees are people, both from the area and from the city, with intimate knowledge of the facts of real estate life in Hough. The board has proceeded wisely but slowly in selecting properties and has developed practical proposals for enlisting financial support from churches and individuals. It has also sought and maintained good working relations with FHA officials, city and national. As a result of this careful background planning HOPE, Inc. was rewarded by receiving the first contract issued by the U.S. Department of Housing and Urban Development under the newly enacted Rent Subsidy Program.

During its first year HOPE has been involved in 5 specific projects in various stages of purchase, renovation and rental. Its first acquisition was a 10-room frame structure at 6516 Hough Avenue, which, since its rehabilitation, serves as the HOPE headquarters. Another small apartment house in the 6500 block has been purchased and 4 of its apartments rehabilitated by volunteer groups. Negotiations for buying and renovating 2 substandard apartments on Belvidere Avenue under FHA 221 (d) 3 provisions were started locally in the winter of 1965 and Washington housing officials were brought into the picture in January 1966. This project became the pilot effort for which FHA made its first rent subsidy grant.

The 21 suites in the 2 buildings of the Belvidere project will be available to low-income families at rentals ranging from $80 to $107 per month. Under Rent Supplement terms the family will pay one-fourth of its income as rent; the difference between that and the "economic" rent needed by HOPE will be paid by the government.

HOPE's newest undertaking is the "400 Houses for Hough" project, sponsored by the Council of Churches of Greater Cleveland and member churches. This program calls for rehabilitation or new construction of 400 adequate dwellings for low-income families, especially those dispossessed through fires and other home damages. "400 Houses" is conceived as a partnership between HOPE, Inc., the Council of Churches, specific local churches and lending institutions, with special roles filled by each. The Council of Churches and denominational leaders will encourage individual churches or groups of churches to participate in the project. HOPE, Inc. will assist in relating each sponsoring institution to a site and provide real estate, architectural, legal and organizational services through its consultants, Land Associates. It will also help identify prospective tenants, negotiating and maintaining relationship with them. A sponsoring church may proceed virtually on its own, assign much of the responsibility to HOPE, or (preferably) act as joint sponsor with HOPE in the whole project.

HOPE believes that if the sponsoring religious institution can provide minimum financing of from $1,000 to $2,000 for acquisition, financing for rehabilitation in the range of $4,000 to $8,000 (or for new construction in the range of $13,000 to $14,000), the balance can be acquired from lending institutions. Certificates of ownership at $5 each are also available to individuals both inside and outside the area. These provide membership in the HOPE organization.

"HOPE's founders consider equally significant as their housing operations the project's other two phases of human renewal and job training," Walter Grevatt emphasized. The human renewal activities reflect HOPE's belief that rehabilitation of property should coincide with rehabilitation of the human beings who occupy it. The job training project (yet to be worked out) will provide to Hough's men and youths on-the-job training in basic construction skills under supervision of skilled craftsmen through work experience in rebuilding the properties.

Stressing tenant-landlord relationships, HOPE's Human Relations Committee will secure an agreement between each tenant and his landlord, listing specific landlord, custodian and tenant responsibilities. Utility companies, city departments and social agencies will help in a home management educational program.

Church relationship with HOPE is provided within the Hough area by the Hough Avenue United Church of Christ and Our Lady of Fatima Catholic Church through their ministers. Mr. Grevatt is chairman of HOPE's board of trustees and its (almost full-time) director. Father Koklowsky is treasurer. The concern of churches and church people outside the area is expressed through the Council of Churches, through local church or denominational financial participation in "400 Houses for Hough" and through purchase of the certificates of ownership.

FAMILY SPONSORSHIP PROGRAMS IN ROCHESTER, NEW YORK

One energetic young lawyer-banker in suburban Rochester with a more than usually sensitive Christian conscience has helped place Rochester high among U.S. cities in volunteer-sponsored rehabilitation housing for low-income families. His name is Francis M. Bradley. He is currently Executive Vice President of the Home Federal Savings and Loan Association of East Rochester and has served as chairman of the lively Ministry of the Laity Department of the Rochester Area Council of Churches.

The genius of the Rochester procedures which Francis Bradley has spearheaded appears to be their flexibility and the development of several optional approaches.

Better Rochester Living, Inc. Nonprofit housing rehabilitation by a church group began in Rochester in 1962 with the incorporation of the organization known as Better Rochester Living, Inc. St. Paul's Episcopal Church advanced to a small group of interested laymen $25,000 in seed money. With this sum BRL began helping families who wanted to own homes but could not raise the down payment.

Mr. Bradley, BRL's vice president, explained to me their use of what they called the "sweat equity" technique, under which BRL locates a property which can be put into livable condition by the work (painting, papering, limited landscaping) of a potential owner. Families desiring to undertake this do-it-yourself rehabilitation are referred from many sources. BRL provides the down payment and closing cost required for purchase of the property, while subsequent mortgage, interest and taxes are paid by the family as rent. The down payment and closing cost are "worked out" by the family through the renovation they are able to contribute, after which the deed of ownership is transferred to the family.

As the BRL transfers title to properties to the families, the funds can then be used on a revolving basis to help a new round of families. Starting from a small credit base in 1962, BRL has accumulated a "line of credit" of $550,000 from the commercial banks through their clearing house and can now handle 55 units at once. At the same time it helps the city's housing problem and rescues from slow decay many dwellings, sometimes blocks of dwellings, in neighborhoods throughout the city.

Family Sponsorship Program. By 1964 Rochester's Urban Renewal Relocation Office and Welfare Department found themselves snowed under by the problem of housing the low-income families, particularly the large ones, being unhoused by the governmental programs.

Reviewing their experience with the large (5 to 15 children) families, these agencies found that such families move more frequently than the average family. This is often the result of urban renewal, or condemnation of the hovels many occupy when someone puts pressure on for more building or sanitary code enforcement. While many large-family problems are internal, the external conditions they face (bad plumbing, faulty electric wiring, dilapidated walls and floors, rats and cockroaches) are enough to unsettle even the most stable relationships. "Such circumstances prove a constant strain on the energies of the adults and require far beyond the normal expenditure of income to maintain even minimal levels of cleanliness and sanitation," says the Relocation Department.

Two years ago Mrs. H., mother of 12 children, was caught in the usual large-family housing trap. Jammed into 4½ dilapidated rooms and unable to find or afford anything better, she said there were many days "when she just hated to wake up." Today, as a result of the pioneering family-relocation program known as Family Sponsorship, Mrs. H. lives on a pleasant street of one-family homes far removed from yesterday's blight. It is a modest 2½ story house probably 40 years old, but it is sound and neat and has plenty of bedroom space; it has furthermore, and unbelievably to the 12 lively children, yard space for the active games of childhood.

The Family Sponsorship program, initiated by Mr. Bradley and Rochester's relocation staff of urban renewal, is essentially a partnership between the renewal agency, the welfare authorities and private citizens and groups interested in providing decent housing for large, underprivileged families. Through this program any individual, civic or religious group may take title to a house and receive rent from the family on a monthly basis. Where the full rent cannot be met from

57

the family income, the balance is paid from welfare or relocation funds. By mutual consent the family guidance help from various agencies is channeled to the family through one assigned social worker. The sponsors also maintain a supportive relationship.

The sponsor takes ownership by paying the down payment and closing costs and he continues to be responsible for the carrying costs of interest, principal, taxes, insurance and maintenance, for which he is reimbursed through the monthly rent. A sponsor finances his part through a bank or savings institution of his own choosing. Methods vary from a conventional or FHA mortgage to a collateral-deposit arrangement whereby the sponsor deposits the down payment and closing costs into an interest-bearing account, thus enabling the bank to offer a 100 percent mortgage.

Operators of the Family Sponsorship program turned for guidance to the experienced BRL group. For promotion it turned also to the Ministry of the Laity Department of the Council of Churches, which became one of the first to buy a house and sponsor a family (and has since taken on two more houses and families). By June 1966, 7 other churches or groups had contracted for sponsorships (Dewey Avenue Presbyterian, Asbury Methodist, South Avenue Baptist, Ekklessia, St. Matthias Episcopal, Society of Friends and the Catholic Interracial Council). Five more were in process, and 10 other suburban churches were actively considering the program.

Rochester Neighbors, Inc., newest of Rochester's nonprofit rehabilitation ventures and its "best hope of a large-scale attack on the large-family problem," involves 15 church-related individuals. It is an interfaith project with 3 incorporators from the Roman Catholic Diocese, 3 from the Jewish Community Council, 3 from the Council of Churches and 6 members at large. Mr. Bradley is chairman.

Already the recipient of a $1 million FHA loan and operating under terms of Section 221 (d) 3 of the Housing Act, Rochester Neighbors, Inc. quickly began to process its first units and is now ready to place 24 families in some 18 dwellings, again scattered throughout the city. This project, too, arranges for a group or individual to sponsor each relocated family. Families are recommended by the welfare and relocation agencies; the Welfare Department and social agencies provide social services; and sponsors bring a more personal relationship. The first round of sponsors (for 24 families) will come from Presbyterian and Methodist Churches and the Catholic Interracial Council.

FHA hailed Rochester Neighbors, Inc. as new in the rehabilitation field and expressed the hope that it would serve as a pilot for nationwide use of the same ideas. Its approach to the dilemma of the large underprivileged family—already widely known as "the Rochester experiment"—follows the principles and methods that have worked well in Rochester's earlier programs. They include: willingness of the Welfare Department to pay the full amount of rent, even if higher than the usual ceiling for welfare clients; close relationship between sponsor and family; selection of houses with enough room and play space for the children; assignment of only one welfare worker to each family; and encouragement of self-sufficiency by the sponsored families.

"There is a bottom to the barrel of large families needing this kind of assistance and Rochester is well along the path of solving a sticky problem faced by most cities," concludes an appraisal account of the city's experience to date.

Churches and Church Members Help. Again it is clear that housing and family rehabilitation in Rochester have been initiated and promoted by its churches. The exceptional combination of 1) leadership from a person of Francis Bradley's knowledge and commitment, 2) the practical, ready-to-help support of the Council of Churches' Ministry of the Laity Department and 3) availability of committed groups and individuals in local congregations, both city and suburban, provides a persuasive example of what the religious forces of a metropolitan community can do, when mobilized, to help relieve any city's pressing family-and-houses rehabilitation problem.

FLOC, INC., WASHINGTON, D. C.

"A vision that has collided with the facts" is one member's description of a unique church-related group committed to family renewal in Washington, D.C. The group is called FLOC, Inc., and its name means For Love of Children.

The organization of FLOC grew out of a determination of Rev. Gordon Cosby, pastor of Washington's Church of the Saviour, and a small band of fellow churchmen on their return from Selma, to "do something" about the dire situation of Negroes in their home city of Washington. At about the same time Washington newspapers carried accounts of unbelievable overcrowding and neglect at Junior Village, Washington's "home" for homeless children. As one writer commented, "though its name is poetic, the Village (where 900 children, mostly Negro, are housed in space intended for 600 or less) is itself not poetic." The stories of the Village conditions culminated in an article in *Harper's Magazine* (November 1965), entitled "A Special Hell for Children in Washington."

The result of these developments was formation of an organization of ministers and lay men and women from 17 Washington churches. Incorporating itself as FLOC, the group committed itself to find "ways to remove at least 400 children from the Village within a year." Working units began on four fronts—locating foster homes, promoting changes in legislation and study of urban problems, providing "group homes" under foster parents, and providing supportive help to reunite families and remove their children from the Village or to sustain families in need and prevent their children from going.

The first "collison of the vision" with the hard facts came to the foster homes unit. A carefully laid out, door-to-door canvass during the spring and early summer (1965) produced an encouraging 174 potential applicants for foster children. The first discouraging fact was the delay encountered in getting the applications considered by an undermanned processing unit at the Department of Public Welfare. Further realism came from the extended list of criteria for applicants as potential foster parents.

In the meantime other groups had been active, and more basic "facts" of work with impoverished and disrupted families had been learned. Clearer also were some of the dynamics of group action by a body of volunteers such as FLOC. The organization hoped that small committed groups would form in many local churches, but they did not.

A change from the original approach, therefore, was in order. The really enthusiastic people were invited to join groups reorganized by function (home rehabilitation, social design, restoration corps, group homes) rather than by congregations. The new membership provided for: *core members* who accept a personal commitment not only to the FLOC mission but to a daily discipline of prayer, training, interpretation, and small but regular financial support; *associate members* who endorse the mission, wish to participate but not to assume commitment and discipline; and *supporting members* who give time and money occasionally but not regularly. This revised organization was functioning as a small but lively group of around 80 "working" members when I attended a training session in September.

Houses have been acquired as rapidly as funds and development help have become available. A notice in the March 17 newsletter posted the good news that "a total of $345 per month was pledged at the FLOC mass meeting of March 7. This allows rental of two houses @ $125, with $95 toward another, either bought or rented." The April 29 letter reported "FLOC Buys Another House"—with a down-payment from the Memorial Evangelical United Brethren Church of Silver

Spring, Md.—and another reunited family took their children out of Junior Village. In May the restoration corps, mission group of the Church of the Saviour, bought a house in northwest Washington, did the renovation, and established a supporting relationship with the family in this home.

Not all the family renewal activity involves housing. Several teams of two or three FLOC members (often from the same church or neighborhood) provide supporting help for one or more families each. These are families, recommended by the welfare agencies or learned about through FLOC churches, who desperately need help of many kinds in order to be reunited or to be kept from falling apart.

"We are not boasting about what we have been able to do for our families," said Kathryn Campbell, secretary of FLOC. "It is unbelievable how much people have to learn about just getting along with each other. We are constantly humbled as we find ourselves trying to shape our families' lives according to our own middle-class standards." With 2 other FLOC members, Miss Campbell is currently trying to help a 16-year-old girl who wants desperately to hold together her family of 6 brothers and sisters whose mother died recently while the father was, and still is, in jail. Two of the teen-age boys have already acquired police records. "We hardly know where to begin with this family, and something basic happens to one or more of them practically every day."

FLOC is also gradually making itself felt in public action. It responded to the report of the District Commissioners on Junior Village with an open letter of protest and suggestion to the commission, which was mailed to all members of Congress and reviewed in the press; testified at public hearings, talked with Appropriations Committee members and sought wide public support for more liberal budget provisions for the Village; and has worked on legislation to provide federal assistance for care of children in foster homes and institutions.

A training course for prospective FLOC members is conducted in 12-week semesters, each one in a different church. Lectures are coordinated by Rev. Fred Taylor, FLOC executive director, and leaders come in from church, civic, social and public agencies also working in rehabilitation.

Most religiously committed of the groups I encountered in the whole anti-poverty field, FLOC is also rapidly becoming one of the most experienced and best-informed groups seeking to bring lasting help to today's distracted and disrupted poor families. Financially, it has operated thus far and will likely continue to depend on privately contributed funds. Some thought has been given, but no action taken, on a possible request for an OEO or other grant to finance more rehabilitated houses, since this, rather than families in need, seems to be the primary delaying factor.

Five churches—Church of the Saviour, National Advent Christian, Fairfax Baptist, Mt. Zion Methodist and Church of the Pilgrims (Presbyterian)—provided the initial leadership of FLOC and have continued to give spiritual as well as material support. Since its launching, the organization has drawn its core and associate members from more than 20 congregations.

FLOC's "collision with the facts" seems in no way to have dimmed its vision. It has produced a tried and tested membership, far wiser, and if anything even more committed, to its purpose to free children and their families from the nightmare of institutional living and to give them a real home. FLOC members are "willing to begin where welfare departments leave off; to make friendship with their families a two-way street; and to change signals as quickly as necessary."

CONCEPTION REGULATING CLINIC, PHILADELPHIA, PENNSYLVANIA

When in Philadelphia in November I learned of plans for the first large-scale, fully equipped and professionally serviced, church-sponsored birth control clinic that had come across my path.

The project, sponsored by the African Methodist Episcopal Church, calls for establishing a Conception Regulation Clinic at the denomination's newly opened Sarah Allen Home in Philadelphia. Actually the clinic is already functioning on a limited basis, and a request for $41,000 of public funding to put it into full operation has been initially approved by Philadelphia's official OEO agency.

The clinic is a special outpatient medical service of the Sarah Allen Home, housed in a modern, 2-story building with classroom facilities, medical examination areas, waiting rooms and staff offices. Professional medical, nursing and nurse-teacher services are provided. The clinic goal is to give patients knowledge of the physiology of reproduction and counsel in techniques for regulation of conception. After examination and consultation, an individualized program of regulation will be established for each patient. A careful plan for patient education and follow-up by a professional staff is also included.

The service will be made available to low-income families throughout the city at a nominal charge based on the patient's ability to pay. Prepared to care for a minimum of 5,000 patients per year, the clinic will be operated in the late afternoon and early evening to meet the needs of working women.

While all welfare and medical agencies will be informed about the clinic and its services, interpretation of the plan to their parishioners by the sponsoring AME churches (some 35 in the area) and other cooperating churches is counted on. A sum of $75,000, most of it from the AME Church, has already been raised for this and other programs related to the Sarah Allen Home.

NEWARK HOSPITAL, EL PASO, TEXAS

In El Paso, Texas, Newark Hospital, supported by the Methodist Board of Missions, maintains a planned parenthood clinic as well as outpatient services for the residents of the area. Nearly 13,000 patients were served by this small hospital during 1966-67, many of them seeking information about the planning of their families. This guidance includes prenatal and postnatal care in the case of parents who are expecting additions to their families.

BEARDSLEY TERRACE PROJECT, BRIDGEPORT, CONNECTICUT

"Imagine yourself the mother of 8 children under 12 suddenly left alone. This is a conscientious mother who truly cares but whose husband had to be institutionalized perhaps for life. The State stepped in to support the children and the mother went to work at night in a hospital. She really wanted to help herself, but she developed a kidney infection and other health problems. This family, now living in Beardsley Terrace, has been without money—or food (except for a few gifts) —since April 5. The State checks have been delayed since March 16 because of her working and the fact she has recently moved. . . . Would your church like to adopt this family?"

Well, would it? It was a good question, put to the churches of Bridgeport, Connecticut, by the Beardsley Terrace Committee of the Bridgeport Council of Churches. On the surface it sounds like the old-fashioned "missions handout" approach, but I learned that in reality it was one development in a 3-year program of realistic outreach to families in a low-income housing development by the council's United Inner City Ministry.

Beginning early in 1964, the program first concerned itself with the project's children of various ages. As in most such programs, however, attention soon turned to the parents and to families with special needs. The main activities have included:

A *preschool program*, referred to as the "Little School," which was first sponsored and financed entirely by the Bridgeport council. It started with a full-time paid director and 27 children (ages 3 and 4), helped during the year by 30 volunteers from the churches and by parents of the children. Success led the Board of Education to finance and expand the program after the first year.

A *recreation program* for older children began for 2 hours after school each day under paid supervision in 2 buildings and expanded to 5 hours a day in 5 buildings, involving 250 children. Three council-paid supervisors are assisted by 20 neighborhood youth workers, and the administrative committee has been organized to include equal representation from Terrace residents.

A *tutorial and remedial reading program* is housed in space contributed by the Board of Education. Twenty-five volunteers from the churches took a 2-month formal training course to be ready for its opening.

A *summer day camp program* for 7- to 12-year-olds is an 8-week recreation and enrichment program, which began in 1964 with 46 children. Demand led to a second 4-week group for another 58. Three directors, assisted by 10 youth corps aides, ran programs in 1965 for 150 children.

Notable progress in the number of children involved and in outreach to the parents has characterized each of these activities, which have also enlisted an exceptionally large number of reliable volunteers from the churches of Bridgeport.

From these accounts, it is evident that many things are being done or can be done to assist families in need not only to acquire decent roofs over their heads but also to find help with health, household management, emotional and psychological problems. Few educational, child development or even job training projects develop very far before they recognize the need to involve parents or whole families in facing, discussing and seeking solutions to day-to-day problems.

Family relocation and rehabilitation housing have enlisted and should increasingly enlist the efforts of church groups. Obviously not nearly enough attention has been given by religious forces to the serious situation of low-income families, especially the many-children ones, as they are pushed from one substandard "home" to another by urban renewal and other bulldozing developments. A few church groups have shown that practical ways can readily be found to help these families with immediate (as well as long-range) housing problems.

What seems to be required of any group seeking to provide rehabilitated housing units for families desperately in need of them is mainly willingness to commit the group's assured credit standing in the community and to provide the time of a committee or director to study the local conditions, determine the best of various ways to meet them and carry out the assigned functions of the sponsoring agency. The most important need is for someone with a knowledge of the real estate, credit and legal options to be willing to take the lead. Local planning or housing agencies are also equipped to provide detailed information and counsel to any group with an interest in this kind of activity.[1]

Direct person-to-person or family-to-family service, often including but going beyond the provisions of livable housing, is also a singularly "churchly" function. Every city of size—and every county regardless of size—is almost certain to have its "hell-spot for children," seldom better and conceivably worse than Washington's Junior Village. The earnest, disciplined effort of many groups, such as FLOC, Inc., as well as the programs for families in public housing units are everywhere greatly needed.

[1] Urban America, Inc., 2 West 46th Street, New York, New York 10036, can provide information and indicate local sources of guidance to any groups with an interest in sponsoring low-cost, nonprofit housing in cities, large and small, across the country.

5 Community Organization

All concerned with the tool of community organization, widely emphasized as a saving instrument for today's hard-pressed inner-city residents, are indebted to Lyle E. Schaller for the comprehensive analysis of what is old, new and most significant about it, in his book *Community Organization: Conflict and Reconciliation.*[1]

The term community organization has been used over the years to describe a wide variety of activities. In recent years it has narrowed in meaning to a method or process of effecting social change.

"In this process," says Lyle Schaller, "the residents of a community are organized so they are able to identify their problems, establish priorities among their needs, develop a program of action and move on to implement this program." This problem-solving activity is usually generated by discontent with current conditions. It emphasizes development of local leadership, recognition of the right of local self-determination of needs and goals, mobilization of local resources and use of democratic procedures.

Should the churches become involved in community organization? Can a good Christian be active in this sort of thing? These are the wrong questions. Today the churches should not be asking "if" but "how" they should take part.

On the "why" of church participation, Lyle Schaller points to the Christian's love of his fellowman and the love expressed by Christians through their church. Community organization, enabling individuals to attain a new sense of dignity and self-fulfillment, helps the church to express this more effectively. The church can also fulfill the unique role among many other organizing forces of keeping the organization process non-self, or neighbor-centered.

[1] Nashville: Abingdon Press, 1966. Direct and indirect quotations used by permission of the author.

Institutionally the church is itself one of the organizations in the community. Fortunately the assumption that the local church exists to serve the people in its community is more and more widely acknowledged. If this principle is accepted, "it is difficult to see how the church can expect to do this without becoming involved . . . in the dynamics of social change in its community."

Ways in which local church groups participate in community organization are described in the following pages.

F.I.G.H.T., INC., ROCHESTER, NEW YORK

"All we want is to have it in writing." A spokesman for Rochester's predominantly black organization, F.I.G.H.T., was binding a bargain with the city's official urban renewal agency. He was also demonstrating his organization's newly acquired self-confidence in how to operate in City Hall politics. For once, his group came armed with the power needed not only to voice their demands, but to get assurance of results firmly recorded "on the dotted line."

Gaining this kind of voice and power does not come easily in any American ghetto community; getting it in Rochester, even after the disastrous riots of July-August 1964, was no exception.

Laying the Groundwork. As frequently happens when rumblings of discontent from the ghetto erupt into violence, confused, conflicting, seldom helpful reactions came from many quarters. When all that these suggestions seemed to contribute was further confusion, a group of clergymen, after extended consultation with Negro church leaders, acted on their conviction that the vital need in Rochester at that point was establishment in the Negro community of an independent, mass-based community organization.

The cooperating clergy group moved first to call in a leadership team from the Southern Christian Leadership Conference. After that organization decided that other commitments would not enable them to give the time and effort required, the clergy group, through the Council of Churches-affiliated Board of Urban Ministry, turned to the Industrial Areas Foundation, the agency directed by Saul Alinsky, whose community organization efforts had made progress in Chicago and other cities.

Before agreeing to come to Rochester, Mr. Alinsky set two requirements: the coming of IAF would have to be requested by the Negro community, and its financing for a 2-year period, at $50,000 a year, underwritten. Three months (October 1964–January 1965) were then spent in an intense effort to raise funds—*first* by the Rochester Ministers Conference (the Negro clergy) in informing and preparing the Negro community; and *second* by the Board of Urban Ministry, backed by the Rochester Area Council of Churches.

The Board of Urban Ministry is structured and financed by the local Protestant denominations, whereas the council is composed of member congregations. Approval and a contribution of $10,000 a year for two years came first from the Presbyterian Board of National Missions, and $4,000 a year was secured from national sources of the Episcopal Church. The Urban Ministry Board then quickly raised the balance from national and local units of American Baptist, Lutheran Church in America, Methodist, Reformed, Unitarian-Universalist and United Church of Christ sources.

The Negro clergy experienced little difficulty in assuring Saul Alinsky that a large segment of the Negro community supported IAF's coming to Rochester. Though no part of the $100,000 2-year budget came from the Council of Churches (and hence from no local congregations), the council's board of directors was asked for and voted its official approval of the invitation to IAF. On April 1, 1965, the IAF staff began to work in Rochester with the new organization named F.I.G.H.T. (Freedom, Integration, God, Honor—Today).

From the first day when citizens, businessmen, many churches and other groups learned that the Urban Ministry was thinking of bringing Saul Alinsky and IAF to Rochester, a "howl of protest" went up. With the help of press, radio and television the clamor was soon heard well across the nation.

The most vociferous antagonism was expressed in the Gannett Press. Attacks on Alinsky, livid accounts of the "doings" of IAF in Chicago, accusations against the Council of Churches and individual clergymen who favored the proposal filled the news pages, as well as prime time on radio and television.

"The city was pretty literally 'shaken to the foundations'," Rev. Richard N. Hughes, executive director of the Council of Churches, recalled to me when I visited Rochester and F.I.G.H.T. headquarters in June 1966. "Though they were badgered from every side—many even from their own congregations—the ministers were not intimidated." With the further help of a few enlightened laymen ("whose power lay outside the political nexus") the Council of Churches, too, held its ground. "We lost a few irate contributors, but actually gained more than we lost, even financially."

Once the Board of Urban Ministry had raised the 2-year budget and the directors of the Council of Churches had given official approval to the program, both the ministry and the council stayed thereafter entirely out of the picture. It was agreed by all concerned that F.I.G.H.T. was to be an organization primarily of Negro people and groups banded together, as its constitution provides, "to unify the Negro people in Rochester, in order that they may assume their rightful role in solving the problems and determining the course of action that affects their lives in this city." "Since the day the agreement with Saul Alinsky was signed," said Mr. Hughes, "the project has been in the hands of the Negro leadership."

Organization and Early Accomplishments. The temporary steering committee decided to concentrate first on completing the permanent organization at a formally called convention scheduled for early July. Minister[2] Franklin H. Florence of the Church of Christ was elected temporary chairman. Saul Alinsky named Edward G. Chambers, veteran IAF organizer, as staff director, and two local Negroes and a third part-time person were hired. This staff then joined the Negro clergymen, church women and other local leaders, in working "around the clock" to secure participation of church groups, tenant groups, neighborhood associations, social clubs, barber shops, youth gangs, etc. in the surrounding neighborhoods.

From the outset Minister Florence announced that F.I.G.H.T. was to be a "black organization for black people." Only assistance, not leadership, from whites was accepted. As he explained, the Temporary Steering Committee faced a big challenge in communicating to the Negro community that F.I.G.H.T. would not be a front by which outside groups could manipulate the community. If for public relations only, F.I.G.H.T. had to take a militant stance from its birth.

By the time the convention date of July 11 arrived, 131 groups had affiliated with the organization. They sent approximately 1,200 representatives to the meeting, of whom 75 were white. Visitors were welcomed, but not on the floor of the convention. With very little change the constitution was adopted providing for 27 area and interest-group vice presidents (from the clergy, block clubs, youth, Spanish speaking groups, etc.); a delegate council of representatives from each organization, plus officers and committee chairmen to meet monthly; and a permanent Steering Committee. Minister Florence was elected president.

The new organization began with a quiet effort to organize groups of dependable youth leaders to be on hand wherever conflicts might be expected to develop during the hot summer evenings. On at least

[2] This is the form of address he prefers, since "Reverend" he considers "not humble enough."

2 occasions, where angry teen-agers had started bottle-throwing and car-window smashing, F.I.G.H.T.'s youth cadres were successful in dispelling the crowds where police efforts were unavailing. After a few instances of that kind and the passing of the rest of the summer without more serious troubles, the police began to see in F.I.G.H.T.—at least in its youth contingent—a new ally at points where they needed all the reinforcements they could muster. Other first-year achievements include:

Picketing the suburban homes of slum landlords responsible for code violations in F.I.G.H.T. neighborhoods, "resulting in correction agreements."

Job and employment activities, involving placement of 275 people in jobs; working with Xerox Corporation's "Step-Up" program; training for Civil Service examinations for police jobs (worked out with Colgate-Rochester Divinity School); requesting $65,000 from OEO for a general Civil Service training program.

Securing recognition of F.I.G.H.T.'s Urban Renewal Committee as the citizens' group that must be consulted in developing renewal plans for the Third Ward; and securing the city's agreement to build new housing *before* demolishing the old.

On the poverty front, making successful demands for opening meetings of the ABC Board (official OEO agency) to the public; for poor peoples' control of neighborhood service centers; and for inclusion of 3 F.I.G.H.T. representatives on the board.

Mobilizing political support for a Negro candidate for city councilman-at-large who carried the ward against opposition of a "white-bossed" Negro machine.

Handling 30 to 40 complaints weekly involving rent, welfare, police, street gangs, etc.

Entering segregation debate with the Board of Education; and working to relieve "open enrollment tensions" at several high schools.

Tensions: Internal and External. F.I.G.H.T. succeeded in giving its supporters in the black community an organized base and a voice strong enough to demand and secure attention from the normally all-powerful white community. Its methods, though forceful (sometimes "rude and abrasive" as promised), were on the whole democratic, constructive and nonviolent. The main problems during the first year were not external, but internal. As one commentator put it, a minority of the original leadership group became concerned about how their own personal interest and aspirations would be affected by what was now obviously a mass organization; others wondered about their own role in the organization; still others saw the organization as a payroll. "Because some of F.I.G.H.T.'s initial leadership group was drawn from the ranks of pre-existing Negro leadership, factions appeared almost simultaneously with its formation."[3]

A further complication lay in the fact that Rochester's Negro population is concentrated in two geographically separated areas, roughly comprising the Third and Seventh Wards. While groups from both sections are actively included in F.I.G.H.T. membership, much of the leadership has come from the Third Ward. I was told in June 1966 by a "noninvolved" commentator (of whom I could find very few) that the organization had not yet "taken hold across town" in the Seventh Ward.

Another and more fundamental issue reared its head as the organization began to make itself felt in matters of housing, education and urban renewal. This is the question of "the polarization of the white and black communities." F.I.G.H.T. was considered by its leaders from the beginning as "of, by and for" the black community. This predominant note was soon heard in "segregationist" demands for low-rent housing in the already heavily Negro Third Ward. Other policy actions reflected the belief of Minister Florence and others in the kind of "black power" that stresses improvement of Negro areas above integration with the whites. The accumulation of tensions came to a head at the second annual Convention in June 1966, where the opposition rallied around a challenger representing a group "unalterably opposed to segregated neighborhoods." While this provided a democratic exchange of viewpoints, the threat to Minister Florence's leadership was overwhelmingly defeated.

Visiting F.I.G.H.T. headquarters a few days after the 1966 convention, I found Minister Florence and the staff ready to go forward with new policies and projects authorized by a series of strongly worded resolutions. These, Minister Florence felt, showed "the large majority of F.I.G.H.T.'s membership enthusiastically in support of the activities to date and ready for new advancements both into and on behalf of the organized Negro community."

Church Involvement in F.I.G.H.T. In our talk about the origin and activities of F.I.G.H.T. Edward Chambers, IAF staff director, emphasized that "there wouldn't be any F.I.G.H.T. without the Negro churches." The organization was made possible actually by an un-

[3] From "Progress Report on the Development of Community Organization in Rochester's Primarily Negro Wards," prepared by Rev. Herbert D. White, director, Board of Urban Ministry, Rochester Area Council of Churches.

71

precedented combination of 1) moral support and approval by the city's overall ecumenical body, the Council of Churches, 2) financial underwriting by the major denominational bodies through the Board of Urban Ministry and 3) indigenous leadership and commitment by the Negro clergy and congregations in the areas of greatest need. So widespread has the influence of the Negro churches been that one writer referred to F.I.G.H.T. as "a brand new religious organization."

Once the IAF was brought firmly into the picture, the Council of Churches and Board of Urban Ministry had no further part in the subsequent activity of F.I.G.H.T. A minor exception was the continued membership, by invitation, of Rev. Marvin Chandler, associate director of the Council of Churches and himself a Negro, on the steering committee of F.I.G.H.T. This was largely a personal relationship and not an "official" connection between the two bodies.

The interest of many white Rochesterians has resulted in the organization of Friends of F.I.G.H.T., a small auxiliary group unique among Alinsky organizations, which has been said to make a stronger attack on the white status quo than F.I.G.H.T. itself. "Friends" activities received the approval of a number of church groups, and its president is a Roman Catholic layman.

The extent to which F.I.G.H.T. itself identifies with its religious community is indicated by the closing statement in its (September 1965) Progress Report that "the bridge between young and old is narrowing. The gulf between the churched and unchurched is closing."[4]

EAST CENTRAL CITIZEN'S ORGANIZATION, COLUMBUS, OHIO

"God has placed us in a unique and extremely visible position to bear witness to Christ and his healing love," said Pastor Leopold W. Bernhard in his 1965 year-end report to his congregation at First English Lutheran Church in Columbus, Ohio. He referred to the

[4] In fall 1966, F.I.G.H.T. entered into negotiations with representatives of Eastman Kodak Company seeking adoption of a job training and employment program for up to 600 Negroes to be selected by the organization. After a plan had been worked out and a covering agreement signed by a vice president of Eastman, the company refused to accept the plan, indicating that it would not make an employment agreement with any one organization and that the officer had not been authorized to act for the company. The company continued in its refusal to work out a training program with F.I.G.H.T. in spite of pressure from that organization, from "Friends of F.I.G.H.T.," and numerous other sources. Several national denominational church bodies, holding Eastman Kodak stock, registered a protest against the company's position at its 1967 annual stockholders meeting. Further negotiations finally resulted in a cooperative working agreement between the company and the F.I.G.H.T. organization.

church's action making possible creation of the East Central Citizen's Organization (ECCO), a pioneering venture into community organization through which a church body, this time a local congregation, has once again taken the lead.

Through ECCO, Pastor Bernhard and a group of loyal supporters within his church have brought into being what is regarded among anti-poverty workers as "a self-help endeavor of the first order." Going back to Thomas Jefferson's idea of "ward republics," ECCO has provided a wholly new approach to maximum feasible participation of the poor which is being watched with great interest by governmental and other anti-poverty leaders across the nation.

ECCO is an incorporated neighborhood foundation open in membership to 6,500 residents of east-central Columbus. It aims to improve the services and general welfare of the community through decision-making by its residents. The area covered by ECCO includes a rapidly growing, low-income population, roughly 70 percent Negro, 25 percent southern mountain whites and 5 percent "native" white residents. In what was once an upper middle class neighborhood, a drastic change has taken place practically in one generation. As described by a Columbus observer: "From the outside, the houses of east-central Columbus . . . look solid and respectable. . . . Inside . . . the two-family structures are bursting with tenants, four kids to a bed. . . . The air trembles with a cacophony of shouting drunks, jazz, auto horns and television. . . . You get a quickly composite picture of despair and neglect among the jobless, the fatherless, the aimless, the hopeless. . . ." But, the story continues, "beneath the neighborhood's flaking crust something else is stirring, too. The people call it ECCO . . . a grassroots attempt at self-government that aims to reverse the kind of tragic decline that is rotting inner-city neighborhoods across the country."[5]

How It Came About. The story began, as portents of change in local churches frequently do, with a serious budget crisis. The church's Neighborhood Center had been established in the first place to meet the pressing need for some kind of community service facility in its rapidly deteriorating area. Use of the Center increased rapidly, as did budgets for trained staff and facilities. Early in 1965 the Board of American Missions notified the church that its annual supplemental grant of $19,500 for that year could not be continued. Help sought from the United Community Fund also met with no success.

During this time Pastor Bernhard spent a brief period at the Urban

[5] "The Meaning of ECCO." Robert Kotzbauer, *WRFD Commentator*, January 21, 1966.

Training Center in Chicago, where he learned of new approaches to community organization "as the major vehicle of social renewal in the months and years of the immediate future." To him, as to Lyle Schaller, the question was no longer, should the church be involved in community organization, but how?

The immediate "how" was answered by bringing into the picture Mr. Milton Kotler of the Institute for Policy Studies of Washington, D.C., who advocated the formation of "a self-governing community foundation at the heart of which stood the transfer of a legitimate agency of social service to the government of the poor under the provisions of very explicit law." This approach applied especially to First Church, where the required "agency of social service," the Neighborhood Center, was already functioning.

To adapt the general proposal to the church and to the East Central community, Mr. Kotler, Pastor Bernhard, the Center staff and several neighborhood residents decided they would need *first,* to secure transfer of the settlement agency to the neighborhood, *second,* to organize a corporate neighborhood foundation to receive and govern the settlement, and *finally,* to enable the new foundation, through funding from various sources, to finance the services and program its members should decide upon.

The first approach (April 1965) was to the church council, which "after much study and soul searching" took the unprecedented step of voting to transfer its Neighborhood Center to the community.[6] It also agreed to help in the formation of the Neighborhood Foundation. Fortunately people of the foundation area, functioning for some time through neighborhood or block organizations, were not unfamiliar with neighborhood cooperation and local decision-making. After consultations within 4 of these groups, and independently in nearly 100 house meetings, interested residents of the area gave their overwhelming support to the project.

Many involved steps followed as the chartering group sought and secured: private funding for the development stage ($3,000 from the Stern Family Fund and $3,000 from the National, Ohio and Columbus Councils of Churches); legal assistance for charter writing (with volunteer help from a member of the Washington, D. C. firm of Arnold, Fortas and Porter); interest and support of OEO and other public agencies, national, state and local; support of Columbus civic, business and church leadership; interest of professional social work and

---

[6] Technically ECCO pays the church a monthly rental, but this is returned by the church to the ECCO treasury. Complete responsibility for operating the Center and its program has been lodged with ECCO.

74

educational agencies; and enlarged neighborhood support through a project leadership council to promote dialogue on needed services and how to supply them.

The East Central Community Organization was born legally with the signing of the final Articles of Incorporation on August 16, 1965. The signers represented the Operating Committee of the Neighborhood Center and elected leadership of the 4 constituent neighborhood clubs. These people formed an interim executive council to govern the new organization until a permanent council could be elected.

How It Operates. Membership in ECCO rests on residence or regular employment within a clearly defined area with a population of 6,500 people. They become ECCO members by signing its roster. By July 1966, 1,500 (or nearly half of those age 16 or over) were already participating. The members form the General Assembly, which meets twice a year and is the general governing authority. It elects an executive council including, besides the officers, 21 elected representatives from the neighborhoods, and appoints an advisory board for help on professional and financial matters.

An interim grant of $12,000 from the Lutheran Board of American Missions helped the new organization through its first "problem" months. Interest of local and national OEO officials, enlisted during the formative stages, led to receipt in December 1965 of a first-year demonstration grant of $100,000 from OEO for "structure and administration" only. Other grant requests have been submitted for specific action programs.

ECCO began with two helpful inheritances from the church's Neighborhood Center. The first was a well-established, community-shared, service and recreation program. The second—derived in part from the Center's previous involvement of local residents—was a substantial corps of experienced neighborhood leadership. The core organizing group of about 40 residents included construction workers, seamstresses, students, insurance agents, businessmen and many who were currently unemployed.

With the Neighborhood Center continuing as hub, workshops, friendship groups and dances are held daily or weekly for third graders through senior high. A Teen Council directs the doings of the older groups, and an active tutoring program enlists the help of high school and college students from all parts of Columbus. The Columbus chapter of the American Association of University Women conducts a nursery school, and a preschool program for retarded children also functions during the school year. Neighborhood mothers have a weekly meeting; older residents have recreation and craft programs. Ohio State University Law School runs a legal services clinic. A sociology professor from Capitol University directs a consumer education program, and a Planned Parenthood Clinic, psychiatric counseling, job placement and welfare referral services are also included.

Of first importance has been a youth-involvement program. For years the only public recreational facility in the area was a roller skating rink, "a racial sore spot" where fistfights and near riots were commonplace. With funds provided by HEW the ECCO youngsters, having rejected one site selected by adults, had just begun, when I visited ECCO, renovation of a rented building of their own choosing with 2 storefronts and 6 apartments. In addition to cooking and some living facilities, the project will provide quiet areas for study and tutorial sessions and space for recreational and educational activities. Through this project ECCO anticipates operation of a racially integrated, youth-managed youth program aimed "to defuse the bombshell of trouble before it begins."

ECCO has also made itself felt at city hall through numerous protests regarding police "incidents" and the usual complaints of housing violations. As a result, City Hall is now coming to ECCO, whose executive council is currently considering a request from the building department for assistance in its code enforcement and from the recreation department for endorsement of an ambitious recreation center. A small staff of community organizers maintains a continuing self-help education and action program.

How the Church Has Contributed. The unique role of First Church and its implications were described by Pastor Bernhard:

"What we have done has suddenly catapulted our congregation into the bright light of public interest in this city, in the state, in the nation, and in the church. All that we will do in 1966 we will do in the glaring light of this interest. And the actions of our congregation will rightly, or wrongly, be taken as the actions of the Church of Christ in this land.

"This is not said in any sense as a boast, but as a statement of fact. Never before has the life of First Church been so critically important. I am fully aware that this poses great difficulties and places on us a responsibility which is enormous. . . . I realize that we might prefer not to be in this position. However, we cannot escape it any longer. . . . Whether or not the Church is the force for justice, reconciliation and peace, is the issue which will be decided very largely by what we do in the coming year."

76

The next pressing question for the church, according to Pastor Billman, the assistant pastor, was: How do we so develop our life as a congregation that we can attempt to be God's colony in this community? A group of 40 members had already begun to study the question.

DOWNTOWN CHURCHES ACTION MISSION, DETROIT, MICHIGAN

DO YOU HAVE A COMPLAINT?

ARE YOU DISGUSTED ABOUT SOMETHING?

Are you sick and tired of your apartment building, your job, the condition of the alleys, rats and roaches, poor police treatment, abandoned buildings, lack of recreation, bad treatment by the Welfare Department?

We're a funny bunch down at the

DOWNTOWN CHURCHES ACTION MISSION

We like to hear complaints, so long as it's about your neighborhood or some of the things that happen to you and your family—something that we can do something about. Don't bother us with the war or the weather—that's beyond our control. Call 962-1100.

Feelers such as this seek to establish contact between ACTION (All Churches Together in Our Neighborhood) and the residents of the "downtown fringe" area fanning out from the back door of Detroit's imposing and influential Central Methodist Church at the corner of Woodward Avenue and Adams Street. This area, considered one of the city's most difficult in terms of human rehabilitation, is known for its large contingent of gamblers, prostitutes, "hoods" and their associates. It also includes a heterogeneous assembly of impoverished families with many children who inhabit the run-down apartments and second floor "flats" over the drinking and gambling enterprises. A ghetto atmosphere prevails.

Here 5 Protestant churches of the area—some white, some Negro and some integrated congregations—have banded together and set up, from their own resources and without benefit of public funds, a small but vigorous community organization called Downtown Churches ACTION Mission.

"Of course, we do other things besides listen to complaints," continues the Bulletin. "We organize neighborhood groups and councils

77

to work on those complaints. And we operate, free . . . a tutoring program, legal aid clinic, crafts and music group (for boys and girls grades 2 through 6) and a vacation church school (for neighborhood children ages 5 to 13)."

A small staff, with some volunteers from the sponsoring churches, succeeded in organizing a community group in the neighborhood surrounding St. Patrick's Roman Catholic Church. Though not affiliated with the church, the group chose to call itself the St. Patrick's Community Council. As a result of this action, St. Patrick's Church enlisted as a sixth ACTION sponsor.

In its first short year ACTION has also organized tenant groups and helped the Community Council conduct community clean-up days and TB x-ray projects. Liaison with the public employment service has helped with job referrals, and the mission is linked with social welfare agencies and social action groups in other neighborhoods. Mutual problems in dealing with slum landlords help to bring together some of the widely divergent groups. Describing special difficulties in trying to work with the "hoodlum" elements, Mrs. Margaret Blessing, ACTION's director, said that most of them had so far remained indifferent, though one group of apartment dwellers succeeded in enlisting even the resident "hoods" in an improvement and landlord-protest effort.

The exceptional challenge of such a situation is obvious, and slow but encouraging progress has already been made.

MID-CITY COMMUNITY CONGRESS, ST. LOUIS, MISSOURI

"The need of a community-in-change is for an organization tool adequate for coming to grips with its problems." Provision of such a tool is the purpose of the Mid-City Community Congress of St. Louis, Missouri. Started by a group of ministers and laymen in May 1966, it was still in the making when I was in St. Louis in October.

The MCCC offers a diverting contrast from most other community organizations. Instead of bringing together people and groups of like interest, economic status and background, it seeks to organize residents, business groups, commercial enterprises, apartment dwellers and owners, of wide diversity—racial, economic, educational and social.

Large portions of its 330 square block area are hard-core slum areas. In addition, there are small but significant sections of middle and upper class whites and Negroes; also small pockets of integrated "neo-urbanites." Still greater variety exists in the business enterprises, which include an upper middle class shopping area; a broad boulevard running the entire length of the area with substantial stores, restaurants and businesses; one of the city's largest health facilities; a large commercial warehouse; and Gaslight Square, a widely known entertainment center. In the ghettos intersecting the area are the usual bars, beauty shops, pawnshops and many small stores and eating places. Housing ranges from upper middle class residential streets, hotels, motels and apartments to slum dwellings and abandoned buildings beyond use even by the most destitute.

In such a setting it is not surprising that the churches also provide striking contrasts, including the St. Louis (Roman Catholic) Cathedral, predominantly upper middle class and white; a small Episcopal church with a "widely heterogeneous" membership; two Presbyterian churches (mostly white); one Lutheran church with a diverse membership and two wholly Negro. A major Greek Orthodox parish, several other "mainline" Negro churches (12 Baptist, one A.M.E. and 2 C.M.E.) and many storefront Pentecostal groups complete the picture.

With this gamut of differing elements and interest, the community MCCC seeks to organize has been well described as "a real microcosm of the entire metropolis . . . [and] like the larger city, it is in extreme distress."

The MCCC Plan. As in other cities, several of the more socially minded churches and a few business groups were trying to do what they could singly to cope with the growing problems. "Their frustration, as they stacked up what they were able to do piece by piece alongside the area's really basic social and economic needs, led to their willingness to participate in the far more inclusive effort represented by the Community Congress idea," said Professor Miller Newton as we ate lunch in an exclusive Gaslight Square restaurant and discussed the contrasting lights and shadows of life in the area— many of them visible through the windows immediately in front of us. Mr. Newton, assistant professor of social science at Webster College, is principal architect of the MCCC plan and its part-time director.

As he explained, the area is in one sense full of organization. In addition to the church efforts, there are neighborhood associations and approximately a fourth of the blocks have some sort of block unit concerned with street lights and other matters of street and property safety. A local OEO community action project and the Urban League of St. Louis (also operating with an OEO grant) provide education, welfare and limited community action services for some of the low-income neighborhoods. Unfortunately none of these programs provides coverage for the area as a whole, and there is virtually no communication among them.

"We concluded," said Mr. Newton, "that there is a deep need for a central, community-wide organization with sufficient power and mandate to plan and conduct a citizen-initiated program for the whole neighborhood." Summarizing MCCC's basic working philosophy, he said, "Every person living, working, conducting a business or owning property in this mid-city has an important stake in its economic and social welfare. If the ghettos continue to deteriorate, the blight will spread. The imminent possibility of that fact alone hangs as a threat over the continued well-being of the prosperous as well as the poor. We believe the sobering results of the creeping devastation already experienced provide sufficient motivating force to sustain an organization such as we have planned."

How do you transform apathy, nonparticipation, anxiety, fear, hostility and small group rivalry into a representative organization for creative community problem-solving? This was the question the MCCC organizers faced. To answer it they have set in motion what they call an organizing process not unlike that followed by other community organizers, which provides for:

1. *Survey and community listening* (to get at "social geography," potential leaders, and "gut issues").

2. *Organization and action of small groups and projects* (result—small groups become formalized and formal groups become aware of a community role).

3. *Organization and action of area groups and projects* (as small groups work together on a larger issue, they interweave the groups, learn about "power deficits" and interdependence. At some point an open-ended temporary council is formed).

4. *Discovery of community-wide issues* (several resulting in desire for combined action are necessary for phase 5).

5. *The first congress* (called by temporary council to form permanent organization, with staff seeking constantly to keep the process democratic and to widen views of participants not used to operating at this level).

6. *Organizational assistance to congress* (staff assists in getting machinery operating and organizers are gradually replaced by program specialists).

How the Plan Works. Maintaining the support of the many minorities involved in its majority requires from MCCC planning that includes the concerns of each group and interweaves them into a common fabric of plan and program for the whole. "This interweaving," said Mr. Newton, "means mutual modification of programs by the

80

concerns of all involved groups." Controversy over neighborhood problems is the life blood of community action, the MCCC's planning prospectus says, "as long as the controversy leads to *a new solution* of the problem rather than to an intensification of alienation between the groups. This "finding of new solutions" is obviously the heart of the matter for an organization undertaking to develop mutuality from such wide diversity.

One example of how this works came out of MCCC's "trial run" during the summer of 1966. As MCCC organizers "tapped" the various neighborhoods they found much dissatisfaction with urban renewal and rehabilitation projects underway or proposed. Limited success resulted from complaints or from active resistance organized or encouraged by MCCC workers. When the frustrations of this piecemeal approach become increasingly evident, however, initial steps were taken with MCCC help to develop with the city housing authorities a master plan to encompass the housing needs of the whole area.

Dissatisfaction of a local printer on Olive Street with his tax assessment led to discovery of a like concern by several business proprietors in the Gaslight Square district, and an Olive Street Business Group was organized. With the support of property owners on 9 strategic blocks of Olive Street, the group met with the Mayor. He promised them tax relief in return for their cooperation in a general revitalization project for the business life of the area. Success not only brought many, frequently warring, business leaders into closer mutuality of action on behalf of the whole community; it has also laid the groundwork for a future, much needed but much tougher, job of revising the entire tax structure of the city and surrounding metropolitan area.

What of the Future? With considerable progress rolled up during 4 short demonstration months (May-August 1966), MCCC's initiating board of directors was assured of sufficient financial underwriting of its first full-year budget, to begin permanent operation on September 1. Mr. Charles Means was employed as full-time staff coordinator to supplement Miller Newton's continued part-time direction, and 3 of 6 authorized full-time organizers were on the job when I visited MCCC in October.

The income side of the budget calls for 20 percent support from 4 local congregations or regional denominational offices—Second Presbyterian Church, St. Louis (RC) Cathedral, Methodist Conference Urban Work Committee and Lutheran (Missouri Synod) District Office; 36 percent from Episcopal and Presbyterian national bodies; and

81

44 percent from local industries and one labor union, the Teamsters. This means that 56 percent will be provided by religious sources and 64 percent will be from local sources, business, labor and religious.

"In-kind" support, such as student help from Webster College (continuing the work of the 14 who participated in the summer "tapping" project) and professional and secretarial staff help and supplies from churches, denominations and business groups, is also available locally. In addition, specialized community service programs supported by Second Presbyterian and Trinity Episcopal Churches (with help from the Episcopal Diocese of Missouri) are integral parts of the total program. As "content" programs develop it is anticipated that the congress may seek public funding for more extensive activities in housing, education, health and other service areas.

Where Does the Church Come In? Local churches or their ministers, with the help of some business leaders, took the initiative in setting the MCCC plan in motion. They also provided the bulk of the small budget for the 4-month exploratory program, and local and national religious sources will continue to be called upon for approximately half of the annual support until the group achieves self-support. The community-service experience of ministers and local church laymen continues to be a sustaining influence in all activities of the congress. This is exercised both through its board of directors and through understanding participation in the local member organizations.

The 4 projects described in this chapter represent 4 distinct methods of approach to community organization, with each one concentrating on community organization as its primary method. In many other anti-poverty programs community organization is an important, though less intensive, method.

Experience is pointing more and more programs, where provision of services has been the basic approach, toward the necessity for some form of direct involvement of recipients of the services. Involvement is first sought for decision-making regarding the services being offered (such as child or adult education, family counseling, health services, etc.). Sooner or later, however, most program operators realize that power to solve many neighborhood problems—police protection, sanitation, building code enforcement—lies almost wholly outside the neighborhood. Effective approach to the providers of these services, centering usually in city hall and "politics," calls for action by the organized voice of the community.

Thus the position of "community service worker," "community liaison," or just plain "community organizer" is appearing more and more frequently in anti-poverty projects, both church-sponsored and otherwise. This means increasing emphasis on the tool of community organization as an effective approach to rapidly deteriorating communities.[7]

[7] Further examples of this development appear in the chapters on farm workers (Chapter 9), comprehensive projects (Chapter 7) and at other points throughout this study. See also the concluding chapter for brief consideration of the "organization vs. service" issue.

6 Economic Development

Without doubt, bringing new industry or other economic activity to an area is an effective and dependable restorer of community health and stability. It is also often the most difficult. Where the development covers a large area and involves provision of such basics as power, water and sanitation facilities, decades of time, thousands of people, numbers of governments (all levels), millions of dollars and unlimited quantities of native persistence are called for.

Where the economic development involves only one community, or the introduction of one plant or industry, the undertaking, though not so time and money consuming, is still formidable. Only by keeping all eyes on the goal of new life and opportunity for the many who will benefit is this kind of victory usually won.

In economic development, as in most other anti-poverty projects, the area's religious forces are usually influential, being frequently in the forefront in initiating or actively promoting such programs. Examples of areawide, local community and single industry projects to which church people have given leadership are included here.

ANTI-POVERTY PROGRAM OF THE CHURCHES IN RURAL OHIO

The rural area of southern Ohio, described as "the grassiest of the grass roots," includes 28 counties officially included as part of Appalachia. For a number of years since the decline of both mining and farming, the grass has been withering and the residents suffering or departing from the area.

"In Jackson County where I come from 11 major industries have closed down or moved from the area in the last 10 years, and our greatest source of income has been welfare," Rev. Glenn Biddle, Field Supervisor of the Ohio Council of Churches' Anti-Poverty Program, told me, as we started a day-long tour of the 5-county section selected

84

for emphasis in the council's anti-poverty program through its Town and Country Department. It is this problem of long-range economic and social improvement in rural Ohio on which the Department has been quietly but persistently at work for the past 12 years. It started in a small way with a grant from the National Council of Churches to sponsor resource development activities in one county. Working since that time with the Cooperative Extension Department and other agencies in support of power dam, water supply, recreation and industrial development projects benefiting many parts of the state, the council's Town and Country Department is now directing its activities intensively to the needs and possibilities of the southern area.

To the T and C staff of two directors (Rev. Clyde N. Rogers and Miss Margaret Brugler), Glenn Biddle has been added as field supervisor of the new anti-poverty program. He is a native son of the area and for a number of years was minister of the Evangelical United Brethren Church of Jackson, the county seat of Jackson County. As a local pastor Mr. Biddle had a major part in the churches' activity in this poverty-pursued locality.

WELLSTON, OHIO

We came early to this small city of 5,700 people where we were to meet Mayor James Rupert, church layman and long-time co-worker with Glenn Biddle in community development in Jackson County. The mayor, we learned, had been rushed off to the local radio station to tell the people of Wellston, of Jackson County and of all southern Ohio the news that the Economic Development Administration had that morning approved the City of Wellston's request for grants (totaling well over $1,000,000) to help underwrite water and sewage facilities for a pending large-scale industrial development.

While we waited for Mayor Rupert's return, Mr. Biddle explained some of the "depression, despondency and despair" in Jackson County in the late 1950's, and the years of cooperative effort by a few local clergy and committed laymen required to put the county back on the road to economic stability represented by the morning's good news.

"By 1959, a number of churchmen became increasingly concerned about the problems they faced," said Mr. Biddle. In December 1960 some denominational leaders, along with the Director of Town and Country Church of the Ohio Council of Churches and Glenn Biddle (then a local pastor), met with the county USDA agent and the regional representative for resource development "to explore and understand the community and church situation in Jackson and Gallia counties."

85

Meetings followed for all ministers of the county and eventually for area leaders—merchants, lawyers, doctors, farmers and labor unionists—with state educators, sociologists, public officials and church executives. Committees on education, industrial development and so on were named and have since helped to halt the economic downtrend.

One recovery milestone was being set in place by the government's approval of the water and sewage grants to Wellston. "This not only will make it possible for us to provide modern water and sewage disposal services to residents over a wide area," Mayor Rupert explained, "it also rounds out our agreement to provide adequate services to the Ralston-Purina Company for its new $6.5 million turkey-processing plant to be built in Wellston." When in full operation this project is expected to involve up to 2,000 workers, including farmers over a 100-mile radius who will grow the turkeys. In addition are the bankers, butchers, bakers, barbers, merchants, and doctors of many communities whose incomes will be restored or augmented as they in turn serve the newly employed people and their families. "I am advised that the Manpower Training School at Jackson is already working with Ralston-Purina on a program to train local workers for the plant operations," the Mayor concluded.

SOUTHERN OHIO MANPOWER AND TRAINING CENTER, JACKSON, OHIO

This most significant of the "new life" ventures for the whole depressed area was our next stopping place. Organized in January 1964 under terms of the Manpower Development and Training Act as "the first Center of this kind in the nation," the school trains a group of approximately 400 students every 4 to 6 months in some 15 job categories, ranging from farm equipment mechanic and farm business manager through machine tool operator, auto mechanic and body repair worker to bookkeeper, stenographer and typist. Sponsored by the Jackson school board, the Center also provides prevocational courses to enable trainees to meet job requirements in their chosen field.

The record of students turned out and the high quality of their performance when hired have given the school a reputation far beyond its own geographic outreach. It has enlisted the enthusiastic support of local industries and has already been a leading factor in the decision of large companies to open plants in the area. The school has also become the pivot point for the rebirth of courage and hope for the people of town and countryside for miles around.

Here again, church influence has been at work, first in bringing the school to the area—through the special effort of Glenn Biddle who learned about the possibilities of such a training program while attending a summer "church-in-action" seminar in Evanston, Illinois—and finally in assuring acceptance of the Center by the community and the opening of homes to house trainees temporarily.

FIVE-COUNTY DISTRICT

Still wider dimensions of the rebirth of southern Ohio came into view in our third visit of the day with Mr. Ralph Moore, area extension specialist and USDA community development agent. Mr. Moore has been in position to plan, promote and help bring into being many of the large-scale development projects which have once again opened the 5-county area to opportunity and hope. As we came in Mr. Moore had been working on charts related to the Jackson County strip of the Appalachian Highway, a new 4-lane artery being financed from federal Appalachian Development funds, matched by the state. "This new road," Mr. Moore explained, "opens up this whole section and means that anything we produce can be shipped anywhere in the world."

Mr. Moore sees his job as "meshing" the area's needs and possibilities through leadership development and the general social action process. A consolidated school, hospital, county planning commission (involving 7 villages, 2 cities and numerous townships), and a rural community water supply program are projects recently completed. "We explain to the banker, grocery store owner or other folks who really run a community what a particular project will do for them and the neighborhood and then they are usually for it. They often don't realize the responsibility that goes with their influence," said Mr. Moore. He also gave credit to churches, particularly some ministers, for help in supporting and interpreting the programs to their constituents.

He and his small staff also work on outdoor recreation as an alternative use of land; agri-business promotion, such as the Ralston-Purina project; water supply and watershed developments, ranging from water supply to a single home or farm to harnessing whole river basins; and cooperation with all public and private welfare and assistance programs, such as health problems, housing studies and help with OEO and other anti-poverty agencies. "Just recently," Mr. Moore told us, "I was able to help a man over in Lawrence County who had a small plot of 3 acres, 9 kids and no money. We contacted the FHA office and in 2 months he got a loan that would enable him to repair and make livable the sub-standard house they had been living in. The joy we saw on that man's face is one of the things that keep us going day by day."

RURAL SETTLEMENT PROGRAMS IN KENTUCKY AND WEST VIRGINIA

For many years home missions boards of the churches have supported mission churches, settlements and schools in the mountain areas of Appalachia. Much good has resulted to the areas reached and particularly to the persons, most often children and young people, fortunate enough to attend the schools or be reached by the church programs. Operating on limited budgets, their resources were totally inadequate for defending surrounding communities against the poverty, ignorance and economic decay which gradually enveloped them.

Though night has long been coming to the Cumberlands,[1] a new day is slowly dawning as the federal government's economic development and anti-poverty programs begin to provide financial help on a scale more nearly approaching the need. Broad, year-round highways are penetrating into and enabling people and products to come out of hitherto inaccessible mountain areas. OEO-supported VISTA and student workers, Head Start, day care and unemployed fathers' programs are supplementing the efforts of struggling local ministers or isolated settlement workers.

Denominational activities throughout Appalachia are being coordinated through the Commission on Religion in Appalachia.[2] At a meeting of the Commission in Knoxville in October 1966 we learned of significant new developments, many still in the planning stage. While enroute to the meeting I enjoyed brief visits at two local missions, each with a long history, and now a changing outlook toward the areas around them.

HENDERSON SETTLEMENT, FRAKES, KENTUCKY

Henderson Settlement is a Methodist mission program whose founder, Parson Frakes, and students "have been preaching and singing their way into the hearts of communities" for 40 years, since its modest beginning as a local church school with 13 children in a crude log barn in 1925. So widely appreciated were the life-long services of

---

[1] Helpful studies of conditions, needs and potentialities of Appalachia and Appalachians are increasingly available. See particularly Harry M. Caudill's *Night Comes to the Cumberlands* (Atlantic Little, Brown, 1963) and Jack Weller's *Yesterday's People* (University of Kentucky Press, 1965).

[2] Address c/o West Virginia Council of Churches, East Charleston, W. Va.

Hiram Frakes, that when the area became incorporated in 1937 the village was named in his honor.

Today Henderson Settlement, an impressive complex of 19 public school, dormitory, work center and other buildings, has, like other settlements in both urban and rural areas, turned its attention from internal preoccupations to the needs and potentialities of the surrounding "up and down" communities.

Under the new (since May 1966) leadership of Rev. Robert F. Fulton, an unusual degree of community settlement cooperation was soon generated by Mr. Fulton's offer to make available for community use a reconditioned fire truck previously reserved for the settlement only. The Frakes Volunteer Fire Company was promptly organized through the efforts of Mr. R. L. Bray, long-time community resident. It has 28 members from the locality and settlement. Sixteen members have attended a training school, and cooperative arrangements for mutual help in case of major fires have been established with neighboring fire departments.

Through its children's home, expanded demonstration farm, preschool program, craft and thrift shop and other new and enlarged programs, the settlement itself employs more than 30 full-time workers. Most of them (with the addition of 5 unemployed fathers under training by the chief carpenter) are from the surrounding area. A forward-moving precedent has been set by the decision to pay all hourly workers at least the federal $1.25 minimum wage and, in the case of permanent employees, to provide pension, health and other benefits. "This has already begun to have an impact on the local economy," Robert Fulton told me with enthusiasm.

A large building is being renovated for use by a wood-working or other local craft industry. Mr. Fulton is spending time during this first year consulting with local residents who have learned to farm the up-and-down terrain successfully, with businessmen in neighboring city areas, with state and county educators and many others who can help Henderson develop a firmly based program of economic and social betterment for the whole section. Gradually he is forming a settlement board of directors aimed at bringing the most informed, committed and competent leadership into directing its program.

RED BIRD MISSION, BEVERLY, KENTUCKY

A half-day's journey from Henderson Settlement is the center and headquarters of the Red Bird District program of the Evangelical United Brethren Church (with over 1,000 congregations in Appalachia).

Red Bird Mission was started as a church and school project by the former Evangelical Church in 1921. The program has grown to include 9 community centers with a resident pastor in each, located in a 5-county area with its hub at the Beverly Mission. Here in addition to the mission's offices are a boarding high school, grade school, craft center and the district's largest and only self-supporting church. Red Bird has also greatly expanded medical and surgical services to a doctor-starved area through a modern, fully equipped 30-bed hospital and a health-mobile service that penetrates "to the farthest end of the five counties," Dr. John W. Bischoff, superintendent of the mission program, assured me.

Through the mission's director of economic development, one interesting experiment, shared cooperatively with a nearby Church of the Brethren mission, has been the operation of a sorghum processing plant. Local farmers grow their own cane and get back from the plant their own juice (less one fifth to cover processing costs). "During the last two years' operation we finally worked out the bugs in processing," said Dr. Bischoff. Unfortunately, however, some newly introduced public programs have provided local farmers with higher returns than sorghum growing, so that project's Brethren and EUB sponsors are in the process of reevaluating it. "We believe the farmers have learned to work together here," Dr. Bischoff said, "and we think something of permanent value can be developed."[3]

MISSOURI DELTA ECUMENICAL MINISTRY, KENNETT, MISSOURI

A large-scale approach to the problems of another geographic area, with a quite different structure and type of church involvement, is emerging in the "Bootheel" area of southeastern Missouri, through the Episcopal Pilot Diocese of Missouri and its Missouri Delta Ecumenical Ministry (MDEM). Here a group of pioneering Episcopal Church leaders began in September 1966 to activate a program to meet the needs of the area's technologically displaced white and Negro farm laborers, "the most critically deprived citizens in the state."

Most of the Missouri Bootheel is rich farmland owned by a relatively few large farmers who have traditionally employed thousands of white and Negro laborers. Mechanization and other advancing farm technology "has obsoleted the services of these people, pushed them into almost total dependence upon welfare and locked them into self-generating conditions of abject poverty," says the initial report of the project. The average educational level is the third grade, with 90 per-

[3] More recent information indicates that the sorghum project is being continued "on a larger basis."

cent in some areas having less than eighth grade schooling. A further complicating factor is "an endemic atmosphere of despair, suspicion, jealousy and distrust . . . [that] has contributed progressively to . . . isolation and breakdown of community."

Socially and spiritually the only natural contacts of the farm workers are in Pentecostal and Baptist churches, whose clergy are themselves mostly untrained and without financial means to tackle the problems. "Although the 'Bootheel' is a prime rural target for the government's anti-poverty program," William D. Chapman, newly appointed MDEM director, explained, "their efforts here have had little impact to date because of inadequate leadership and because the programs seem threatening to both rich and poor alike." Mr. Chapman, an Episcopal priest with broad experience in India, also brings to this assignment familiarity with the other economic problems of Missourians gained from participation in the Delmo Corporation, a pioneering cooperative housing and community development project supported by the churches in another section of the state.

Drawing upon the resources of the church—"perhaps the only agency with a reservoir of trust sufficient to overcome the enormous barriers of suspicion, jealousy and apathy that are present"—the program is aimed toward ecumenical involvement of the Pentecostal and Baptist church groups in the self-reclamation process; toward organization and training of an "MDEM Cabinet" of local leaders; development of adequate housing; and promotion of new agri-business industries and cooperatives suited to the conditions and capabilities of the Bootheel area. Approximately $25,000 is being provided through the Episcopal Pilot Diocese of Missouri for an initial 15-month period.[4]

COOPERATIVES AND CREDIT UNIONS

Moving still farther south we come to the Lafayette and Lake Charles area of Louisiana. There, a far-seeing Negro Roman Catholic priest, A. J. McKnight, and a group of enthusiastic supporters have made economic self-help a reality for people of traditionally low or little income over a wide section of the state, through the Southern Consumers' Cooperative and Southern Consumers' Education Foundation.

[4] The Diocese of Missouri is one of several designated by the Episcopal Church as Pilot Dioceses for experimentation with various types of church related anti-poverty programs. More recent developments in the Bootheel have included OEO funding of a Missouri Associated Migrant Opportunities Program (MAMOS) (see Chapter 9 for description of similar program in Indiana) and formation of the Bootheel Agricultural Services, Inc. Cooperative (BASIC) for growing, harvesting and marketing 200 acres of okra.

Southern Consumers' Cooperative, using the democratic one man—one vote principle, is representative of an increasing number of co-operative enterprises through which people with low economic potential as individuals are, by pooling their efforts, creating new and expanding opportunities for gainful employment and income development. Currently listing more than 1,000 low-income families as members, the SCC conducts a bakery and a loan company, making loans up to $500 to members at low interest rates and operating basically like a credit union. While the bakery is not yet fully self-supporting, the loan fund has been very successful, paying members a 4 percent dividend in 1966. Savings invested in SCC increased from $10,000 in 1963 to $80,000 in 1966. "Through this process our members feel a sense of ownership and control," says Father McKnight. "Many are given their first experience in democratic procedures."

Another cooperative venture, organized by the Selma (Ala.) Inter-religious Project under the direction of a local Episcopal priest, is the Freedom Quilting Bee. Here women of the area, working part-time at a "living-wage hourly rate," earned a total of more than $11,000 during their first year of operation in 1966.

The Credit Union at the Roman Catholic Church of St. Paul and Augustine in Washington, D. C. is the oldest and most widely known of the many successful credit unions organized among low-income families by Catholic churches or parish groups. This "basic instrument of self-help," organized more than 10 years ago by a small group of church members with an opening savings balance of $153, has since then made 3,000 loans totaling $1,175,000 at a nominal interest rate.

A still prospering Protestant-sponsored credit union at Fourth Avenue Christian Church (Disciples of Christ) in Columbus, Ohio was formed in 1958. Beginning with 22 members and $76.75, it had, as of September 1966, 135 members. Loans totaling $151,118 had been made to 335 people and the current share balance was $25,552.

Other credit unions are functioning as helpful components in a number of church-related anti-poverty projects (mostly Roman Catholic in origin). My feeling, however, is that church-related programs in poverty areas, particularly Protestant ones, are not making nearly as much use of this effective tool as its self-help, self-education potentialities warrant.

ONE-COMMUNITY OR ONE-INDUSTRY PROJECTS

Substantial help to many people can result from introduction of a single, going-concern enterprise in an otherwise deteriorating neighborhood. This again is no easy undertaking, and it can safely be assumed that success, where achieved, has been the result of the alert, patient, often self-sacrificing efforts of one determined person or a small group enlisted by him. The influence of local churches or some of their powerful members is usually counted upon to help support such projects and interpret them to the community.

ELECTRO-TECH EDUCATIONAL CORPORATION, GREENWOOD, SOUTH DAKOTA

Electro-Tech is a training and employment project aimed at helping the large Indian population of the area become more employable through acquiring better manual skills. The corporation, involving from 20 to 30 persons at a time in its training process, is largely the result of concern for the "utterly desolate Sioux people" on the part of William F. Fahsing, an Episcopal priest who serves 2 churches and 3 chapels in the Yankton Sioux Reservation area.

Before his call to the ministry, Father Fahsing had been an engineer in television development. Radio and TV devices he produced for his own apartment in Greenwood attracted the attention of Bishop Conrad Gesner, and together they developed the Electro-Tech plan.

The church contributed a building and supplied light and heat. Father Fahsing collected old radios, toasters and vacuum cleaners. These, plus a few donations of cash from friends moved by the idea, formed the working equipment of the training program, which began early in 1963 with 10 local people, ages 16 to 50. As their skills developed, it became possible to produce marketable small instruments. Contacts with electronic industries resulted in a modest first contract with the Farrall Instrument Company of Grand Island, Nebraska. Thus, in February 1965, the Electro-Tech Educational Corporation was organized and the training concentrated on turning out products under the contract.

Continuation of the Farrall and addition of several small subcontracts soon made it possible to operate an actual assembly line and give full-time employment to 8 of the locally trained people. Each one works 40 hours a week at $1.40 per hour. Other money earned from the contracts is put directly into capital improvements and more equipment. "As they complete the training course more and more people can be employed—and more contracts solicited," said Father Fahsing, volunteer project director. No salaried persons are involved, and no federal, state or local funds (thus far) have been used. Besides the building, church sources, such as the bishop's discretionary fund and Episcopal parishes and missions in South Dakota and New York, have financed the other limited expenditures.

"Call it the church in action, call it a sociological extension of practical Christian ministry, or any other high sounding phrase . . . what it boils down to is a private war on poverty for Dakota people on the Yankton Sioux Reservation, waged by the Episcopal Church," said a local news reporter.

TEACHING MEN TO FISH AT GREENPORT, LONG ISLAND

Describing the wide-ranging program of C-A-S-T (Community Action Southold Town) from "seeds sown in (the) North Fork (of Long Island) Ministerial Association," Rev. Arthur C. Bryant, pastor of St. Peter's Lutheran Church of Greenport, says:

"One day two Negro boys disappeared while out on a scalloping boat seeking to earn some money for Christmas. At that time we became aware of a need to provide training for men in the fishing industry. Since the business has been segregated for many years, the poor in our area have no one to teach them the method used by other men to supplement income in the nontourist season.

"As a follow-through on this accident, Mr. Gerald Rocker (a neighborhood aide with Suffolk Economic Opportunities Commission) and myself were sent to Boston to study the Atlantic Fishermen Union's MDTA training program for fishermen. We returned and recommended such a school for this area to serve the entire state of New York. . . .

"However, statistical problems have hampered our efforts. When boats have moved away from a port because of a manpower shortage it becomes very difficult to explain to a government office that there is still a manpower shortage even though the place of employment is away temporarily. And yet, CAST has made some progress. . . . Publicity brought in $100 from a group of students at Yale, and . . . caught the attention of the Dean of Suffolk Community College. If all goes as expected, an extension course in marine life and fisheries will be provided in Greenport for the uptraining of existing fishermen with a tuition fee of $15. Scholarships will be provided for indigent men by CAST, using the funds from the students at Yale."

YUKON, PENNSYLVANIA

Here a local church, Grace United Church of Christ, acting largely through its pastor, Rev. George R. Geisler, joined other community forces in a major plan of economic rehabilitation of a once-prosperous mining community in Western Pennsylvania, where "the mine was finished and all that remained were huge piles of slag and red-dog, a coal tipple, a few naked stone buildings, and some empty coal cars sitting on a siding."

94

George Geisler gives credit for starting "the way back" to the local Lions Club, which worked through its Industrial Development Committee on every angle of what it takes to reverse a community's downward economic spiral and put it on the road to recovery.

The committee learned early two positive steps. *First,* "find out what you have to offer industry." *Second,* "make your town an attractive and inviting place to live in." After a good look around, they found real assets—an abundant water supply, railroads, natural gas lines, electricity, some beautiful land surrounding the town and "above all else, men who wanted to work." The second step was far more difficult, but a "three-year Clean up, Paint up, Fix up Campaign finally produced a clean-faced Yukon with widened and resurfaced streets."

With substantial help from a public utility and a neighboring bank, local promotion efforts attracted the attention of Westinghouse Electric Company, which finally chose Yukon as the site of its first industry-owned atomic testing reactor. The International Paper Company of New York followed with a plant furnishing employment opportunity for 150 to 200 men and women.[5]

Two other instances of local enterprises started by clergymen with economic vision, which came into my purview, were the Richford Enterprises, Inc. of Richford, Vermont, and the Sequoyah Carpet Mills of Andarko, Oklahoma. At Richford, Father George St. Ong, priest of All Saints Parish, and a group of men from surrounding towns, introduced a hockey-stick factory, housed in a prefabricated, quonset-like structure, "erected in a couple of days." Though it has taken much more effort and time than that to make this a going concern, in the area much in need of economic development, the business has progressed to the point where it has been purchased by a much larger manufacturer and established on a permanent basis, with a working force of 25 to 30 local employees.

Donald J. Greve—licensed Methodist minister, city council member and successful local businessman in Andarko, Oklahoma—was recently honored for these latter achievements by receiving the "outstanding small businessman of the year in America" award from the National Council for Small Business Management Development. This award was given in recognition of his successful efforts in launching a carpet factory designed to give employment to many hard-core unemployed Indians in Andarko, center of an area of extreme poverty.

[5] A recent communication from Mr. Geisler says that both the International Paper Company of New York and Westinghouse companies have "greatly expanded their facilities and have employed beyond our expectations."

The company has not only provided employment (often their first steady employment) for up to 300 on-the-job-trained Indian workers; it also provides a profit-sharing plan, free hospitalization, life insurance, legal counsel, a fund for short-term loans, a scholarship fund for employes' children and a department that has helped in building more than 100 homes for the workers on a nonprofit basis. As of November 1966, the firm was building a second carpet plant in Andarko to employ an additional 350 workers, and planning a new furniture manufacturing plant in Elk City to provide over 1,000 jobs.

While large-scale economic growth programs, such as the southern Ohio development, appear to be operating more widely in rural areas and involving a number of small communities, clearly there is need and widespread opportunity for more concentrated efforts in cities, both large and small, for citywide or even neighborhood economic rejuvenation, given an enthusiastic leader or group with commensurate vision, drive and organizational acumen. Many more Yukons, Electro-Techs and Sequoyah Mills, as well as rural area development programs, are obviously called for.

7 Comprehensive Centers and Programs

There is an ingredient in every life which must be found if people are to be worth anything to themselves or their community . . . and they will find it and call it DIGNITY.

—From Statement of Purpose
Fellowship Center, St. Louis, Mo.

At the forefront of religious efforts for and with deprived people and areas are the large and comprehensive community centers and citywide programs. These programs are organized and supported by single denominations, by groups of denominations and by councils of churches; also in more localized areas by a single congregation or combination of congregations. They represent what may be called the more "massive" of the churches' anti-poverty activities.

In spite of great diversity, one thing all clearly stress in common is the search for ways to help all men to find *dignity* for self and family.

The projects brought together in this chapter are of many types. Their programs, though directed toward a common goal, seek to reach it by different routes, with differing combinations of techniques. I have grouped their impressive but "unruly" profiles under three umbrellas—community centers, "ministries" and "parish" programs, and projects by church congregations (singly or in combination of two or more).[1]

[1] In this study, the overall and many sectional projects undertaken with notable success by church groups in New York City have been omitted, not because they are not significant or effective but because they are so numerous and varied that at least an entire chapter would be required to cover them. In the other largest metropolitan areas—Chicago, Los Angeles, Cleveland and Detroit—only specific projects are included, not citywide or broad sectional activities.

COMMUNITY CENTERS

Under pressure of changing inner city and poverty-war realities, many church-sponsored settlement houses—often with venerable records of service in deprived city areas—are shifting from building-centered to community-centered activities. While the buildings are still important focal points, total programs are directed outward toward the people where they are and not just concentrated on those who come to the centers' doors.

WESTMINSTER NEIGHBORHOOD ASSOCIATION, INC., WATTS AREA, LOS ANGELES

Located in a section of greatest need in the nation, this project has grown, says Rev. Archie W. Hardwick, its director for the past 7 years, "from a social agency into a multi-functional agency more capable of meeting the deeper and broader needs that we recognize in the Watts community." Its program, initiated and supported by the Presbytery of Los Angeles and the Presbyterian Board of National Missions, focuses on families, because its sponsors feel that "the only way to understand young people today is to have contact with their families."

Serving this largely Negro community of 70,000 residents, the WNAI program has three broad areas.

The social service program relates to the individual—"his response to society and society's response to him." Through referral it puts people with problems into contact with programs and resources that can help.

The youth training and employment program, financed by OEO, is designed to give 650 youths between 18 and 21 basic education and orientation to the world of work. This second-largest Negro-administered program in the U. S. (next to HARYOU ACT in New York City) uses 30 community aides to recruit and maintain relations with the trainees. Its present staff of 16 teachers, all Negro and all (but one) college graduates, have been recruited through the local (Negro) newspaper and WNAI friends. Each teacher and aide is a full-time, salaried worker and receives six weeks of intensive training.

The community action program, also functioning with OEO and HEW grants, employs a coordinator and 13 aides who, in less than a year, have organized 37 neighborhood councils with a nucleus of 20 active community leaders per council. These groups meet monthly in

98

individual homes to consider neighborhood problems. The officers of the Councils come together in NOW (Neighborhood Organizations of Watts), meeting quarterly (or on call) to sponsor joint action on community-wide problems, such as unsanitary conditions in the Giant Food Market, cleaning up vacant (and burned) lots, or tree planting. Fifty-five local residents were trained as voter registerers. A WNAI field worker is treasurer of a flourishing credit union operated by the Westminster Neighborhood Improvement Association. The staff of WNAI has increased from its original 2 to a current 102, and volunteers (particularly students, but also many from local churches) help at many points.

"Westminster Association is expanding under the impact of two strong pressures," said Archie Hardwick. "One is the urgent needs of the people and community; the other, and increasing, one is the structures of society who want to channel resources into the community to help meet those needs. Westminster is one of the few agencies in Watts which can bridge the gap between these two forces."

FELLOWSHIP CENTER, ST. LOUIS, MISSOURI

"A place to go . . . something to do . . . someone who cares" describes the three United Church of Christ Neighborhood Houses in St. Louis, of which Fellowship Center is one. "All the difference in the world for people with no place to go . . . nothing to do . . . no one who cares."

Fellowship Center came into being in 1943 as a settlement house under sponsorship of the Evangelical and Reformed Church. From the start, it has stressed development of better interracial and intercultural relations. When its earlier location was swallowed by a new expressway in the mid-1950's, Fellowship's present building was constructed and its current, outreaching program began to develop. The Center is located across the street from the multi-unit Cochran Housing Project.

Fellowship's basic support is divided, with approximately 60 percent from United Church of Christ sources and 40 percent from St. Louis' United Fund. Very recently it has been designated as one of several Neighborhood Stations of the Human Development Corporation (official OEO agency) and an allotment of federal funds has made possible needed additions to staff and services. Rev. Louis Huber is administrator of the three UCC Centers in St. Louis and coordinator of the Carr-Central HDC Neighborhood Station, which includes two of them.

Some 40 groups bring regularly to the Center 500 grade school chil-

dren, 200 teen-agers and well over 200 adults. With one worker assigned to every 2 buildings at Cochran, a staff of 7 to 10 (employed
part-time from the area) visit every family at least once a month.

A corps of neighborhod aides are developing community organization units in the housing project. Representatives elected by the building groups come together in a Tenant Relations Council. A Neighborhood Advisory Council unites leaders from the Tenant Council
with others from the whole Carr-Central District.

"We have developed a complaint process that really works," said
Miss Jan Gates, Fellowship's program director. As a result more and
more adults (men especially) are participating in the tenant organizations. "People are excited when they find they get action (even
from the Housing Authority) without picketing."

The Fellowship staff find themselves wearing three hats as they
operate the Center program, take an active (sometimes frustrated) part
in the city's Human Development Corporation, and supervise the
work of graduate students in social work from St. Louis University,
Washington University and Eden Seminary. Volunteers and neighborhood young people contribute "hundreds of hours of service" in practically every phase of the program.

Christ-in-the-City United Church, though separate in operation, is
the newest addition to the Center complex. It was dedicated in November 1965 "to bring the church to the people . . . [and] to make
religion relevant to the life in a troubled, deprived area."

SUSANNAH WESLEY COMMUNITY CENTER, HONOLULU, HAWAII

Under the direction of Mrs. L. Gladys Lang, Susannah Wesley is another settlement house and children's home, with a 50-year history of
distinguished service, which has recently revolutionized its outlook
and approach to a rapidly changing community.

Turning first to 3 low-cost housing projects in the near neighborhood, the Center began early in 1964, before the official poverty war,
to set up study halls and tutorial programs. It also opened the community's first nursery school at the Kalihi Valley housing project under a trained Samoan teacher, wife of a Samoan minister.

When OEO programs became available, Susannah Wesley was the
first to get one underway in Hawaii, opening in June 1965 a school
for 60 youngsters in Kuhio Park Terrace, the area's new high-rise "ver-
tical slum." Later 5 more were added to give a "new look at life" to
180 children in the Kamehameha Home project. A summer program
guided 40 teen-agers through a critical period in their lives and resulted in each of them returning to school in the fall. Eight children

enrolled in a day camp specializing in a United Nations program to widen their horizons.

An interest-finder questionnaire to parent-teacher groups in the housing developments resulted in discussions dealing with health problems, child care, mental health. A home economist has developed classes in cooking and (with the help of a mental health specialist) discussions of family behavior problems. The city's Department of Education has been encouraged to bring adult classes in English and high school equivalency subjects to people in the projects, and the Center's community action program has added cooking, sewing, ceramics and other arts and crafts.

Turning the first "graduation" of preschool youngsters into a community "pot luck" celebration, the Center welcomed "the greatest turnout of parents in its history." One "diploma" receiver explained proudly to his teacher: "My daddy is here, and he's not drunk today." "In fact," said Mrs. Donald M. Kinch, former president of its governing board, "our program at Susannah Wesley has changed the whole atmosphere in the housing developments."

The support of the Center, including the "in kind" portion of the OEO projects, comes from Methodist mission funds and Woman's Division contributions, both local and national. Construction is already underway to replace the 5-year-old building with more adequate quarters.[1]

PRESBYTERIAN NEIGHBORHOOD CENTER, KANSAS CITY, MISSOURI

This project is the most closely church-connected of those I visited. The Center facilities were included as part of the new church building erected by the First Presbyterian Church of Kansas City in 1958 on the site of the original church, which dated back to 1886. The early church, declining in membership along with the changing neighborhood, was without a full-time pastor from 1949 until its reestablishment, with the aid of the National Board of Missions, in 1958.

With the help of a small core of devoted women, an administrative committee, part-time secretary and part-time janitor, Rev. Kenneth S. Waterman, its first and continuing pastor, began the challenging assignment of gathering a community-based congregation and making it into a "serving" church.

From their vantage point in the heart of a changing, low-income, largely Negro area, Kenneth Waterman and his "workers" (now including some 59 members of the church with assigned full or part-time duties) pioneered in developing numerous programs and ser-

[1] The Center's new buildings and facilities were opened early in 1967.

101

vices that have since become widely accepted poverty war activities. They included one of the earliest youth employment counseling and placement servics, a legal services clinic, adult education programs and a Center credit union. The church has a current membership of 120, of which one-fourth are white and three-fourths Negro, approximately the ratio in the community.

In 1964 the Congregation and Center joined forces with the neighboring First Congregational Church to form the United Inner City Services, combining the finances, facilities, administration and employed staffs of both congregations in an enlarged outreach into their shared community. A culmination of this "ecumenical venturing" has now been reached in the historic decision of four denominations to unite into a single new church, St. Mark's, to serve the entire area. Participants are the Episcopal Diocese of West Missouri, the Roman Catholic Diocese of Kansas City–St. Joseph, the Western Association of the Missouri Conference of the United Church of Christ and the Kansas City Presbytery.

Emphasis in the new church is to be on "a strong, united, indigenous Christian community," and its overall goal "a fellowship with separate sacramental ministries having a high quality social service program . . . dealing with the crucial issues affecting the community." Each denomination will provide one full-time member of the ministerial staff. The church will open near the end of 1967 in a new $400,000 structure. It is anticipated that its combined resources will make possible, in addition to greatly expanded worship and religious education services, communitywide programs in home care services. "St. Mark's will be truly a peoples' church," said Kenneth Waterman.

"MINISTRIES" AND "PARISH" PROGRAMS

Councils of churches in a number of cities are waging concentrated, citywide wars on poverty. Some local or regional denominational offices have also provided areawide anti-poverty staffs and activities. Another structurally unique response to growing inner-city tensions are the interdenominationally sponsored "parish" programs.

MINISTER OF METROPOLITAN MISSION, HAWAII CONFERENCE, UCC

"Mr. Poverty" was what they called Rev. Lawrence S. Jones everywhere I went in Hawaii. Employed by the Hawaii Conference of the United Church of Christ to help local inner-city and suburban ministers and congregations "to develop strategy for witness to metropolitan needs," a UCC Minister of Metropolitan Mission serves as listener,

102

catalyst and general "enabler to action" throughout his area. A few random sentences from Larry Jones' recent report of activities skim the surface of what he "gets into" in one month's time.

"The Palama Inter-Church Council (UCC, Methodist, Episcopal) is on the verge of incorporation and the three ministers have worked closely on the OEO pre-school program . . . (as) chairman of the Honolulu Community Action Program Committee (the City's official anti-poverty board) I am currently serving as something of a mediator between Inter-Church Council, pre-school staff and some of the OEO staff. . . ."

"Several members (of our Housing Task Force) sit on the Governor's Ways and Means Committee (on Housing) which I chair and which is just completing recommendations to make moderate income housing more feasible in Hawaii. . . ."

"Things have begun to jump at City Hall in regard to the Community Renewal Program, largely due to aggressiveness of the new director with whom I work as Chairman of the Advisory Committee. . . ."

"We were successful in getting CRP to contract with the Honolulu Council of Social Agencies . . . to do long range planning for 13 target areas. . . ."

"We have continued to operate our Volunteer Tutoring Project under an OEO grant (funded for 60 youngsters and reaching 110)."

"My other major involvement has been in leadership in various workshops for the Community Action staff. . . . (and at the present time) I am . . . preparing a presentation on Power, Conflict, and the 'Aloha' Spirit."[2]

This report might be duplicated with differences of emphasis but similarity of outreach by the 11 other UCC Ministers of Metropolitan Mission located in cities with a substantial number of United Church congregations across the country.

EAST OAKLAND PARISH, OAKLAND, CALIFORNIA

"All the people of the Parish (are) busy with after-school programs, jacket clubs, pre-school programs, JFK School for Dropouts, food, clothing, money, pickets, nurses, doctors, lawyers, people, people— *not program but people.*" . . . Keeping its focus on people, East Oakland Parish provides many daily activities directed toward relief of the

[2] Larry Jones writes that, with the coming on the scene of George Lee for the Episcopalians, the two of them with William McClellan, Presbyterian, are structuring a joint urban mission to include Methodists, Lutherans, Disciples, Roman Catholics and the Hawaiian Council of Churches.

galling needs and tinder-box tensions of a substantial sector of Oakland, a beleaguered American city.

EOP is a nonprofit, church-created corporation in which 7 denominations have covenanted to become "one parish ministering to persons in the area from several centers of service." Participating denominations are Christian Churches (Disciples of Christ), Church of the Brethren, Episcopal, Lutheran (LCA), Methodist, Roman Catholic and United Church of Christ.

The extent of the Parish's influence and of the grave situation within its area came through to me as Rev. John H. Frykman, pastor of St. John's Lutheran Church and EOP president, and Miss Cheryl Arnold, an able assistant, described the Parish activities and the racial unrest in Oakland, which was corroborated by riots and near-conflagrations in the days that followed.

That the situation did not flare out of control is due possibly in larger part than is realized to the intense 2-year efforts of the Parish's many programs for and with the area's teen-agers and older youths. The work of only 2 full-time staff members is extended by part-time services of 30 University of California students, OEO funded up to 90 percent under a work-study program, with the 10 percent balance paid by the Parish. Half of the student workers penetrate specific neighborhoods "getting to know the people . . . attempting to identify problems facing the community . . . (and) acting as catalysts" in organizing groups to search out solutions. The other students are resource leaders advising "jacket clubs," helping up to 60 youths reconstruct a large (Disciples-donated) summer camp, involving many younger boys in sports activities, working with a welfare rights organization, conducting study and tutoring centers and guiding local groups in producing a news sheet.

A distinctive contribution of EOP has been the organization of the John F. Kennedy School. In cooperation with Father Everett Chandler, principal of St. Elizabeth's High School, the Parish set up this special institution, dedicated to answering the question "Can 'kickouts' (from the public schools) be equipped and motivated to find and fill useful places in society?" A $25,000 grant from the Rosenberg Foundation enabled the school to open with 3 full-time teachers, a counselor and 5 work-study student teachers. Its beginning enrollment of 26 soon increased to 70 and is still going up. The school has recently been separately incorporated as a nonprofit educational institution.

EOP takes an active part in official anti-poverty programs in the area. Three of four area advisory action councils have been chaired by men related to EOP. This tie-in with publicly supported programs has not, however, silenced the Parish's "prophetic voice" of activity, since it has consistently sought to stimulate participation by the poor of the area and protests against adverse public actions.

Seeking similar purposes though by different organizational routes, parishes are in various stages of development in West, Southeast and North Oakland.

CHURCH-COMMUNITY ACTION PROGRAM, PORTLAND, OREGON

C-CAP was first organized in Portland's greater Albina area where 80 percent of the Negroes of the city (and virtually of the state) live. Seeking "a more intensive and realistic involvement of the churches in the life, needs and challenges of the community," C-CAP was backed by an initial contribution from the Oregon Methodist Woman's Society, by further funding from churches of the Portland Presbytery and the Presbyterian (USA) Commission on Religion and Race and by the coordinating efforts of the Greater Portland Council of Churches.

The organization opened three pre-Head Start nursery schools, which were later turned over to the public school OEO program. A modified preschool program has also been started by C-CAP in a neighboring public housing project. Eight college students volunteered full-time services and many others part-time for a summer community involvement program. More than 100 men and women from participating churches have become VEAPS (participants in the Volunteer Education Assistants Project), and serve as volunteer tutors and teacher-helpers in public school classrooms.

One year after C-CAP's founding, 12 churches of another congested area started a similar program called East-CAP, and the two CAP's share the services as director of Rev. Paul Schulze (minister of the Lutheran Church—Missouri Synod). Mr. Schulze also described plans for HUB-CAP, a third church-coordinating program for downtown Portland with special outreach to skid row-ers, homosexuals and young adults working or living in the area. "This is involving the old-line, downtown churches, the very heart of our Protestant and Catholic forces," said Mr. Schulze.

PROJECTS BY LOCAL CONGREGATIONS

While many anti-poverty projects described in this study have been started by, or have at some point involved single church congregations, most of them have been related to some larger program undertaken either denominationally or through a council of churches. A few particularly courageous congregations, however, have generated and continue to operate their own full-scale, anti-poverty programs.

105

Due to space limitations readers will have to construct, from between the lines of the brief accounts that follow, the real story of what each project has required from busy people in terms of determination, willingness to experiment and patience with slowly emerging results—in short, of stout-hearted Christian commitment to neighbors in need.

IMMANUEL UNITED CHURCH OF CHRIST OF LOS ANGELES, CALIFORNIA

This small congregation, located on the northern edge of Watts, was organized as a semi-rural church in 1907. Occupying its present building since 1931, the church served lower middle income white people until they began to leave the racially changing neighborhood after World War II. In 1961 the building was turned over to the local UCC Conference, and plans were made to foster a new, indigenous church to meet the challenge of the now predominantly minority neighborhood.

The congregation now numbers 50 members (with 40 in average attendance). Tutoring, job training and other work with youth have resulted in bringing into the church house 3 of the most active gangs, now merged into one locally helpful, instead of destructive, group called The Deacons. The program also covers a year-round nursery school; fun clubs and other programs for grade schoolers; a planned parenthood clinic; community organization of block councils; and participation by the ministers and others in local public agencies.

"Believing in the priesthood of believers, we like to think that our church has 40 ministers who minister to a parish of several hundred," Rev. Speed B. Leas, its pastor, assured me.

PALOLO METHODIST CHURCH, HONOLULU, HAWAII

Palolo Methodist is another local congregation working, with some help from denominational sources, to establish a "Christian presence" in one of the most needy and difficult public-housing areas of Honolulu.

Through what it calls the Palolo Community Project, Palolo Church contributes its educational facilities, nearly half of the time of Glenn Murray, its Christian education director, and many hours of volunteer participation of its members in a wide-ranging program to children, youth and adults of the area. A year-round preschool program serves 4- and 5-year-olds, with the help of OEO funds and a number of community mothers. An after-school remedial program and evening study hall give a lift to 90 to 100 fifth through ninth graders. "Our opportunities are great," said Glenn Murray, "and we are set to expand them as rapidly as our resources—from church or government sources—make possible."[3]

RIVERSIDE INNER CITY PARISH OF DETROIT, MICHIGAN

The Inner City Parish is the diversified, dynamic, inner-city ministry of Riverside Lutheran Church. In 5 years, under the leadership of Rev. David Eberhard, the church has quadrupled in size and financial resources. With the help of state and national Lutheran boards, it has recently built a new chapel and church house.

Riverside's unique contribution to its changing area is its Inner City Community Clinic, staffed by 80 professional men and women volunteers. On two evenings a week teams of specialists give medical, legal, dental, psychiatric and social welfare help, as well as spiritual, marriage and financial counseling.

The national Lutheran Inner City Peace Corps provides several student workers (paid $85 a month plus room, board and transportation by the Synod) who help to administer a community youth center, a welfare center for distribution of food, clothing and furniture (operated as a "co-op" store) and a tutoring program for elementary and high school students. Youth Village, another pioneering venture to provide 10 to 12 "homeless, hopeless and neglected boys with love, guidance, security and a disciplined home environment," was just being implemented (with a $50,000 grant from a suburban church) in October 1966.

Each project is separately incorporated and operates with its own board of directors, responsible for administration, policy direction, recruitment of personnel and financing. Support is sought from congregational, denominational, community or individual donor sources. The pastor with the help of a full-time staff of 9 to 16 members provides overall supervision.

DORT-OAK PARK NEIGHBORHOOD HOUSE, FLINT, MICHIGAN

An "oasis of concern" in a "desert area of need" in inner-city Flint, the Neighborhood House came into being because "following their study of the book *The Changing City Challenges the Church* 3 women felt compelled to put what they had learned into action." As often

[3] With its OEO funds "cut," the church, through the Division of National Missions funds, will pick up and continue the recreation project and will try with local funds and volunteer help to carry some of the remedial program, writes Glenn Murray, indicating the kind of belt-tightening determination to carry on shown by numerous church-connected projects when faced with cuts in public funds.

happens when a few start looking into what can be done, these women found 2 ready allies—the director of Dort Community School, who "dreamed of having a house where . . . girls might (be taught) actual homemaking practice," and Oak Park Methodist Church, which gave the use of a house it owned near the school.

Starting with the simple purpose "to fill whatever community need we are able to fill and to help people help themselves," the Dort-Oak Park project has expanded rapidly from a summer, then year-round, daily church school (started with 3 and now using 18 biracial volunteer teachers) to an adult program enlisting parents in reading improvement, homemaking, better preparation for parenthood and a variety of community services. A recent count showed as many as 190 people coming to the House in one week's time.

"Because our project is the first of its kind in our area, we have had little precedent to guide us," said Mrs. C. D. Arrand, president of the Dort-Oak Park Neighborhood Council (and former president, United Church Women of Flint). Operated initially with volunteer help from the church, the center is now also served by local businessmen, residents of the Dort community and people from other churches across the city.[4]

These are all stimulating programs in their areas and stimulating to write about. They are highly pertinent to this study, *first* for their evidence of varied, intense, productive, increasing outreach to impoverished people across the nation, and *second* for their record of "life and substance" involvement of church people as "servants" in the name of their Servant Lord.

[4] Representative of the "upward bound" trend reported by many of the projects visited, Mrs. Arrand since writes: "Many more teachers are involved—easily 40 (instead of 18). . . . Designated an Advance Special of our Conference, we are beginning to get some financial support from our (Methodist) District, Conference and National Mission Board. The Planned Parenthood Association is using a room at the House for an out-clinic as is the Human Relations Commission. . . . A class to train nurses aides . . . has over 60 names on a waiting list. . . . Our teachers and leaders come from 24 different churches representing 13 denominations. . . . We are making plans to have a full-time coordinator-director." (*Author's note:* It all started with 3 women who read a book!)

108

8 Welfare Recipients

Let us hope that today's poor continue to be noisy and unaccommodating. As soon as they become deferential we shall know that the poverty war has been lost. For it is the spunk of the poor, not the charity of the rest of us, that will win it in the end.

Harvey G. Cox[1]

The recent Report of the President's Advisory Council on Public Welfare, entitled "Having the Power, We Have the Duty," says that needy people, "as the most defenseless segment of the population, are in the greatest need of special protection." It is ironic, the report continues, that it is precisely this group that, too often, has the least protection "along with the least of everything else."

Under mandate from Congress, the Council carried out a broad, 2-year examination of the public assistance programs for which the Social Security Act authorizes federal funds. It also recommended sweeping changes in the total welfare administration process now shared so "chaotically" by federal, state and local agencies. Assessing results of the present program "caught between overwhelming needs and inadequate resources to meet them," the Council concluded that "public assistance payments are so low and so uneven that the government is, by its own standards and definitions, a major source of the poverty on which it has declared unconditional war."

Three basic recommendations of the Council, among many others, were *first* that adequate financial aid and social services be made available to all who need them *as a matter of right; second,* that a floor of required income be established for each state in terms of a modest but adequate budget to serve as the minimum level of assistance that *must* prevail; and *third,* that need be the sole measure of entitlement.

[1] "The Ungrateful Poor," in *Christianity and Crisis,* August 16, 1966.

109

The Council took a strong position regarding the provision of assistance as a matter of legal right, stressing the fact that public welfare is the only governmental program operating today that has the task of providing an ultimate guarantee against poverty and social deprivation. The very concept of a guarantee, the report adds, requires that it be available on a dignified basis as a matter of legal right. "Today our public welfare provisions fall short on all these counts." In fact, concluded the Council, "a guarantee which is not supported by adequate, nationwide requirements and financing is—*in the realities of Modern America*—no guarantee at all." (Italics added.)

While the National Advisory Council was listening to men and women from all levels of involvement at public hearings across the country, contacts of anti-poverty workers with the day-to-day realities of life on public welfare "in Modern America" were leading them to agree emphatically with the Council's conclusions. "We couldn't say it better than the Council did, i.e. 'that present variations in the levels and scope of income guarantee are unconscionable by any measure,'" one worker assured me.

This widespread dissatisfaction with the negative contributions of public assistance to the War on Poverty has produced a growing movement to help relief recipients show their spunk by organizing and raising their attention-getting voices against "the system" that does little but hold them in poverty. Action on this new front has been eagerly engaged in by church-related battlers for and with the poor. In the pages that follow are brief descriptions of several programs of organized protest in which church groups and leaders have taken part.

The Advisory Council on Welfare also stated that "recently the concept of legal entitlement to public assistance has received new emphasis through rulings of the Federal Government and the growing interest of the legal profession." An example of a substantial program of legal aid to families in poverty, representative of many being conducted under church auspices, is also included here.

OHIO'S STEERING COMMITTEE FOR ADEQUATE WELFARE

1. In Ohio, the sixth richest state in the Union, 275,000 citizens "on relief," because of insufficient appropriation of state welfare funds, are trying to live on an average of only 74¢ per day for all food, clothes, school expenses, transportation and personal needs. This is not quite 78 percent of a minimum standard for health and decency established (by the State Welfare Department) on 1959 living costs.

Many church bodies and other organizations, including the

110

Ohio Citizens Council for Health and Welfare, have declared themselves in support of grants at 100 percent standard for health and decency based on the cost of living.

Will you support appropriation of the necessary funds for such a standard if elected to the state legislature?

2. Most families on public assistance face an immediate critical need for good winter clothing for their children, which they cannot meet on the above budget. Yet our state finished the last fiscal year with an officially reported surplus of $51,000,000.

What emergency action will you take when the new legislature convenes in January to deal immediately with the problem of clothing for *this* winter?

The Ohio Steering Committee for Adequate Welfare put these questions to all 1966 state legislative candidates and gave wide publicity to their replies. The questions highlighted the crucial need for at least the "1959 minimum" monthly relief grant and the "crisis in clothing" needs for children entering school in the fall—dramatized earlier by welfare recipients at the state capitol in Columbus.

In Ohio nearly 250,000 people are dependent on the state's "economy" relief programs. The move to bring public attention to their plight began early in 1966 when "a group of like-minded individuals from the churches and the social work profession emerged to work with the welfare clients," Rev. Paul Younger, of Cleveland's Protestant Ministry to Poverty, explained on my visit in late October.

Through PMP, which he helped to organize, Paul Younger and a small nucleus of other leaders sought contacts with similar groups in other Ohio metropolitan centers. Following a workshop with client and nonclient participants from 8 counties in January 1966, each county set up an organization which later formed the Ohio Steering Committee for Adequate Welfare.

The first joint undertaking of the OSCAW was the 10-day "walk for decent welfare" in June 1966, in which relief recipients and their sympathizers converged on Columbus from various parts of the state. They aimed to dramatize the fact that, with a substantial balance in its treasury in the offing, the state was still holding its monthly relief grants (for both federal and state programs) 30 percent *below* the amount the state welfare authorities had indicated as a minimum family budget in 1959 (when living costs were considerably lower).

Much publicity was generated during the walk in which a small core group, such as the 35 welfare mothers and children who made the entire 155-mile walk from Cleveland, were joined for short distances by sympathizers in each town and city on the way. The walkers were also the butt of abusive demonstrations, and in many towns support from church groups was conspicuously missing. Some 2,000 people finally gathered on the steps of the state capitol on June 30 to urge Governor Rhodes to call a special legislative session to raise relief grant levels to 100 percent of the 1959 minimum. Every leading church denomination made a policy statement in support of the 100 percent welfare grants and followed it up with participation.

Though the march did not bring an increase in grants it did highlight for Ohio citizens that the state's treatment of its indigent poor was "unconscionable by any measure."

The September 20 issue of *Ohio Adequate Welfare News* said that, in response to parents' requests for funds for school clothing with winter just around the corner, "a $5 grant has been issued to a number of clients. Too many clients did not receive any additional funds." Another delegation of 85 welfare clients and supporters from Akron, Cincinnati, Cleveland, Columbus, Lorain, Toledo and Youngstown again went to Columbus in a vain attempt to give the governor a request for an adequate allotment for school clothing "out of the (estimated) $51 million state surplus."

A third campaign "intended to shock citizens of Ohio into increasing welfare payments" consisted of 4 advertisements in Cleveland's 2 daily newspapers, drafted and paid for by the Council of Churches of Greater Cleveland. The third full-page ad of the series ran on December 24. Under the caption "Merry Christmas, kids" appeared the picture of a rat. The text said: "You were expecting reindeer? In some sections of Cleveland rats are very 'in' this year. Nearly every kid has one. Sometimes two. In some parts of Cleveland rats actually make out better than people. At least they eat better."

Earlier in the month a picture of a pregnant woman with her hand resting on her stomach was followed by the headline: "Let 'em starve." The text pointed out "It's not that we're in favor of letting children go hungry. . . . We just don't want Cleveland to squander a lot of money on worthless welfare cases. Like the 73 cents a day we give every child on public assistance. Whether they deserve it or not. That's right. 73 cents a day. If the kid's not careful he can blow it all on lunch. . . ."

While none of these programs resulted in improving the lot of relief clients, they did several other significant things. First of all, they helped to make millions of "nonrelief" citizens of Ohio aware of "the realities of life in modern America" faced by fellow citizens dependent upon state welfare grants to keep body and soul in some kind

112

of miserable togetherness. Participation in OSCAW organizations also brought new hope, self-confidence and the lift that comes from raising their own voices in protest to thousands of victims of "the system."

Finally, people of conscience were forced to take sides. While much (often virulent) opposition was expressed, friends and sympathizers also came forward from many quarters, frequently the churches, and brave souls among them formed and continue to provide the bulwark of the Adequate Welfare groups.

PENNSYLVANIA'S CRUSADE FOR CHILDREN

In Pennsylvania a similar program, organized by the Greater Philadelphia Council of Churches, resulted in a statewide Crusade for Children with a march on Harrisburg where state appropriations committees were considering the 1966-67 "relief" allocations.

"The combined thought, prayers, skills, work and walking of many people from many concerned groups resulted in a trek of 10 bus-loads of people from Philadelphia and neighboring communities to Harrisburg on June 8," said Rev. Jerry Carpenter, C of C director of Community Services. The Philadelphia caravan was joined by delegations from Pittsburgh, Chester, Lancaster and Scranton. Maintaining contact through its leaders with key legislators during the summer months, the Crusade, through publicity, persuasion and demonstration, helped to bring about a $15 million increase (about $5 a month per person) for families on AFDC in Pennsylvania for the ensuing year.[2]

THE WEST SIDE ORGANIZATION AND WELFARE UNION OF CHICAGO, ILLINOIS

"WSO held a community meeting in the cold, roach-infested headquarters at 1527 West Roosevelt Road. It was the revival of the town meeting in an urban setting . . ." and this is the difference between the West Side Organization of Chicago and many other poverty-area community organizations. It is an organization of people, as individuals, not of other organizations acting as their representatives.

WSO members meet every Wednesday night to discuss problems and possible solutions. Out of these meetings have come the WSO tutoring programs, basic adult education classes, a teen leadership program and direct action campaigns to meet a variety of neighborhood crises.

The idea for this organization "by the people" grew out of experi-

[2] A more recent report notes that the Crusade led to formation of the Philadelphia Welfare Rights Organization and its affiliation with the National Poverty Rights Organization.

ences of some staff members and students of Chicago's Urban Training Center for Christian Mission with local leaders from the city's West Side areas. One writer has said: "At its rawest, the world of the West Side is the world of the hustler. Pimps and prostitutes, junkies and pushers, gamblers and thieves, wineheads and slick talk artists comprise one segment of a society forced to exist on the inversion of human values." Fortunately these are not all. Immigrants from Mississippi and Alabama, the old sharecropper, the young teen dropout, the mother with 10 dependent children, the unskilled laborer displaced by a machine, the aged poor—"these, too, belong to the West Side community."

Two-man teams, with one member each from UTC and from the area, spent several months meeting and talking with people of every kind and station. The eager response resulted in the formation early in 1964 of the West Side Organization for Full Employment.

The WSO constitution provides for individual memberships at $2 per year (waived in case of ADC families), for a governing Community Meeting (weekly), and for a board of directors of 21 to be elected by the Annual Community Meeting. The staff consists of an executive director, associate director, 3 organizers and the editor of *Torch*, its rapidly expanding community newspaper. Students from the Urban Training Center are assigned to work with the WSO staff for 3 to 9 months, as part of their training.

The first WSO budget was underwritten by the Urban Training Center, Chicago City Missionary Society and the United Church of Christ Board of Homeland Ministries. A substantially increased budget for 1966 has been partially covered by an estimated $15,000 income to be raised by the organization itself, from dues, benefits, etc., and a contribution from the Stern Family Fund, a foundation in New York.

Early efforts concentrated on job finding (resulting in placement in good jobs of about 500 people formerly unemployed during these first 2 years), and on attempts to upgrade the employment of Negroes in businesses in the area. "A sharp rebuff in its efforts at this latter point," Chester Robinson, WSO director, explained to me, "made us realize the need to become a mass membership organization if we were to make ourselves heard and felt in any effective way."

One important step toward this mass movement was the assignment of teams to work in the multitude of storefront churches throughout the West Side. According to Rev. Robert C. Strom, WSO Chaplain, "WSO spread the word in a thousand ways." It also concerned itself with the immediate needs of ghetto families. "If there was no heat, a bucket of coal was carried in. If there was no food, a collection was taken. If a family was illegally evicted, they were moved back in. . . . Slowly the suspicion diminished that WSO might be one more subtle attempt to exploit the neighborhood." At the same time the confidence of the staff, drawn from the neighborhood and with little previous experience of this kind, began to grow. "Some had had prison records," writes Bob Strom. "Yet they worked 12 and 14 hours a day, many times without pay. The reason—an impotent community was starting to move toward power."[3]

WSO was also becoming painfully aware of the immense influence over the lives of West Side residents wielded, frequently in open violation of law, by the city's Department of Public Aid. Besieged daily with complaints of unfair, punitive actions by case workers, checks suspended indefinitely without regard to food or housing situations, subjection to intolerable work relief requirements, WSO one day in the spring of 1965 "reached the end of its patience." In response to a particularly flagrant case, 30 people from WSO staged a first sit-in at the District Office of the Department of Public Aid. They sat until their demand for restitution of money believed rightfully belonging to a fellow-member was listened to. When the result was a prompt payment of the withheld funds, "the news spread rapidly through the West Side grapevine," and led to organization of the WSO Welfare Union.

Responding as to an idea whose time had come, the WSO Welfare Union, a special action group within the parent organization, flourished from the day it was formed, building block groups around issues defined by welfare recipients and processing grievances through WSO's already tested procedures. During its first year the Union showed a record of more than 600 successfully processed grievances (actually 1,300 since WSO began). It has already organized 4 other locals across the city, with headquarters of 3 of them located in churches of their areas.

While WSO has met its share of setbacks, attacks and harassments, it has continued to grow both in membership and community-wide effectiveness. Poverty-related groups in Chicago and other cities are studying WSO's experience as they, too, seek to develop the Welfare Union idea.

In relation to the churches, WSO began with and maintained the support of an important segment of Chicago's Protestant leadership. It continues to serve as an eye-and-mind-opening training ground for ministers and other students from the Urban Training Center, whose

[3] "Last Rites for Liberals," Renewal, February 1966.

director of community training, Rev. Archie Hargraves, is the elected president of WSO's board of directors. The United Church of Christ Board of Homeland Ministries also continues its support of WSO. On location WSO works closely with at least 35 storefront congregations in the West Side area, and area churches have been among the first to offer help to welfare union locals.

"For the poor, the means of obtaining justice for themselves is the same means that every other group in America, weak or wealthy, has sought and used: *Organization*," says Kenneth Waterman. "The organization of the poor themselves, by themselves, will be their vehicle of responsible citizenship and the real alleviation of degradation and poverty."

LEGAL ADVICE CLINICS, CHICAGO, ILLINOIS

During the Spring of 1964 a group of Chicago lawyers decided that there is need in the Chicago area for legal assistance to persons without knowledge or means to obtain a lawyer. "We concluded further," says their letter requesting approval of the plan by the Chicago Bar Association, "that the many churches located in neighborhoods (of the poor) throughout the city are in a position to help meet this need by offering legal assistance as a part of their general ministry."

As a result of their deliberations 15 lawyers began in the summer of 1964 a ministry of legal aid under a Legal Advice Committee in the Social Welfare Department of the Church Federation of Greater Chicago. Operating as the Legal Advice Clinics with 8 volunteer lawyers for each clinic location, the program began at 2 local churches. By the end of the first year 6 clinics were functioning and 6 more have since been added, with more than 120 lawyers currently involved. Each lawyer serves approximately once a month, as teams of 2 lawyers staff each clinic for 2 hours on a regular evening each week. A waiting list of some 30 lawyers makes it possible to set up new clinics as rapidly as church locations become available.

Though they function from a church base, the program is not restricted in any way to church members, either lawyer volunteers or clinic users. Clinic services include giving advice, direction and in certain instances complete representation. A clinic lawyer follows up his advice, when necessary, with phone calls or letters on behalf of his clinic client. Between June 1965 and June 1966, 583 clients were handled by the clinics. Experience with the kinds of inquiries and situations dealt with has shown that less than a third have required help beyond the clinic.

Reporting to the Chicago Bar Association on early experiences with the clinics and clients, the 15 initiating lawyers cited a number of needs: 1) for education, for both lawyer and client, to avoid bringing "a greater wealth of good intentions and confused gestures than of sound advice"—and to help the client who was inclined to believe the disc jockey who promised unlimited time to pay for the stove, or not to understand the value of keeping a carbon copy of what he signed, or not to know that she had any rights at all against a vanishing husband; 2) for communication and interpretation of legal documents, to fill the "gaps" such as those between what a contract says and what the purchaser thinks it says; and 3) for concern, since "the foremost need of anyone with a problem is someone to talk with who really cares about him and his difficulty."

The Church Federation's central committee recruits the lawyers to man the clinics, and the recruits profit from a monthly session (usually a long lunch hour) where problems are discussed and important public agency heads are brought in for clarification of procedures, legislative requirements and attitudes.

When I visited the clinic headquarters in October 1966 the staff was working on a plan to expand the clinic idea to the suburban areas of Cook County surrounding the city through a new nonprofit, OEO funded agency, to be sponsored jointly by the American Civil Liberties Union, the Community Renewal Foundation (concerned with low-income housing) and the Church Federation.[4]

Thus churches and their members are reaching out to help "the most beleaguered victims of the poverty struggle: the recipients or should-be recipients of public aid." Sometimes the initiative has come from local congregations or from the denominational level, sometimes from councils of churches, either separately or in cooperation with other community organizations. Legal counseling services are being undertaken by councils of churches or by one or more parishes within a neighborhood area.

A sense of common purpose, unity of action and a nationwide exchange of experience and knowledge in work with welfare recipients are now provided through a new national organization called the Poverty/Rights Action Center with headquarters in Washington, D.C. Dr. George Wiley, former associate director of the Congress of Racial Equality, heads the new group. The National Council of Churches joined other religious, welfare and labor groups in securing financial and membership support.

[4] I have since been informed that this proposal has been funded and that 6 offices will soon be providing full legal services in areas of greatest need around Chicago.

117

Joining planners of the Ohio March for Adequate Welfare, the Washington Center urged welfare recipient groups across the country to send delegates to the Ohio March or to stage demonstrations in their own cities on the concluding day, June 30. Approximately 18 smaller demonstrations were held in cities across the country. The Poverty/Rights Center then brought 100 leaders of these groups to a meeting in Chicago in August, where "for the first time, welfare groups began to have the feeling of being a national movement." The Center was asked to continue as coordinating agent, and a national advisory committee was named.

The President's Advisory Council on Public Welfare called for all public welfare agencies "continuously to seek greater public understanding of their programs, methods and objectives through all appropriate means." With the help of the churches and other like-minded groups, welfare recipients themselves are already making a substantial contribution, not only to more equitable administration of public assistance programs, but to the greater public understanding of the facts, complications and frequently "unconscionable" injustices of our public welfare system.

If they are to "come to life" constructively on their own behalf, these most neglected of God's children greatly need the kind of understanding, encouragement and help which church people are in a singular position to give. In any community, church people, when acting together, are the most influential civic or political group. There is no doubt that they can, by joining forces with those in need, end both the punitive attitudes and demeaning (often self-defeating) regulations that make a mockery of the (so-called) "welfare" system in "Modern America."

9 Farm Workers and Indians

"Indiana's migrants have poor health, poor diets, poor housing, poor clothing and a poor physical environment. . . . They lack the educational key to success, and they exist on the lowest rung of the economic ladder. . . ." No matter how many times or ways you describe it the story of the migrant group in any state or community comes out stark and grim.

Difference in detail but little difference in outcome is shown also by the story of American Indians, especially where they have left the reservations and moved into urban communities.

During well over 50 years since their plight first became a matter of national attention, while the rest of the nation has been making rapid economic advance, the condition of seasonal farm workers has steadily retrogressed. Powerful forces kept from these workers the protections and aids to progress extended by law to other workers. As a result their abysmally low economic and social status has continued in spite of concerted efforts by thousands of people and groups, many church-related, to improve these conditions. A similar though smaller-scale effort has been carried on with a minimum of results to improve the economic status of our Indian fellow citizens.

PROGRAMS FOR MIGRANTS

In recent years a few encouraging things have begun to happen to migrants. Some small gains in Social Security, passage of the Migrant Health Act in 1962, repeal of P.L. 78 with its annual influx of competing, low-cost Mexican labor, some advances in education and finally a breakthrough (though only for a small number of workers) in the extension of the national minimum wage protection to workers on very large farms.

Another historic breakthrough occurred in 1966 in California. Here hundreds of grape workers in the Delano area of California, after 11 months of bitter hold-out, finally won collective bargaining agreements with 2 of the nation's largest growers, the Schenley and Di Giorgio Companies.

Thus, nearly 60 years after attention first focused on the sad condition of these workers, whose labors continue to provide the rest of the nation with its essentials of food and fiber, an aroused public opinion has finally spurred some concrete improvements. One further important happening was the inclusion of Title III-B in the Economic Opportunity Act, "to meet some of the special problems of rural poverty . . . of low-income rural families and migrant agricultural employees and their families." By this action Congress finally came through with cold cash in place of the usual pious platitudes.

THE CALIFORNIA MIGRANT MINISTRY

Much has been seen, heard and written about the 11-month strike of seasonal farm workers in the grape-growing area of Delano, California. Not so much is known of the ongoing work of the churches for, by and with agricultural workers throughout the lush valleys and other fruit and vegetable crop areas of the state.

Activities of the California Migrant Ministry for the past decade or longer have been directed toward improving the life—which means attempting to lift the burden of poverty—of the state's thousands of seasonal farm workers. In contrast with migrant ministries in other states, the California Ministry (for a number of valid reasons) has not contracted for the use of public funds.

Referring to the developments at Delano and the eventual acceptance of bargaining by the Schenley and Di Giorgio Companies, Rev. Wayne C. (Chris) Hartmire, CMM director, said that "the strike and winning of collective bargaining is basic to any attack on the poverty of farm workers in California." As collective bargaining relations are being worked out with the Schenley Company, "a whole new atmosphere is being created. Both sides are doing everything they can to make it work." Hourly rates of $1.75 to $2.00 (plus incentives) have replaced what had been $1.25 to $1.40. A grievance committee is functioning, and union shop provisions for membership and dues collection are a part of the contract. The company is already attracting "the cream of the labor crop," and worker morale is at its highest.

While direct responsibility for worker organization and conduct of the strike was carried by the labor groups, primarily the National Farm Workers Association (NFWA), it was clear, according to Chris Hartmire, that "the strike could not have lasted without the support

120

of the church." This support held firm under heavy pressure from many sides only because of the tireless effort of the CMM, both in understanding support of the workers and in persuasive interpretation to the churches. Support through the Migrant Ministry came most directly from the churches of Northern California, which sustained the greatest opposition. Involved also were state denominational leaders.

Though the initial anti-poverty effects from collective bargaining will be felt first among the grape harvesters, these developments are certain to raise the economic level of workers in other areas and crops. This spread will be neither automatic nor rapid, however, without much further help with education, organization and the encouragement that workers from the churches can give. Plans for strengthening these services constitute the 1966-67 program of CMM. Its main features are four.

1. *Maintaining MM presence with the NFWA in Delano.* This is important because (a) farm workers are still relatively weak in relation to employers and the community power structure; (b) the church's presence in Delano is a powerful witness, for it is costly and farm workers know and appreciate this; (c) concretely the church's "being there" has helped to minimize violence, to reduce the estrangement of workers to organized Christianity and to bring a measure of independence and judgment to the movement; and (d) support from the churches has strengthened the farm workers' position within the labor movement.

2. *Continued consultative support to denominational rural projects.* These include congregational ministries, community organizing and other services in numerous Lutheran Church in America, United Church of Christ, Baptist and Methodist churches, along with local migrant ministries in several farm-worker areas.

3. *Introduction of worker-minister teams.* For this new form of ministry, young clergymen and theologically articulate laymen will be recruited to serve as "worker ministers." They will live in rural fringe neighborhoods and work as farm laborers with projected earnings of $1,500 per year. A supporting denomination will provide an additional $2,000 per man. The total income will not be large enough to cut the worker-minister off from his fellow workers, but the denominational subsidy will free him enough to engage in organizational activities. The CMM feels that the worker-minister can be a vital link between the life of the church (local and regional) and the life situation of his fellow workers.

4. *Continued interpretation and leadership among churches and community.* CMM plans to continue its work with local migrant min-

121

istry committees. The summer program will be continued to strengthen year-round efforts and reach out to new areas and forms of ministry. Interpretation to the church of conditions and issues related to farm workers and support of state legislative and other public developments are also among the continuing responsibilities.

The hard-won success of California's seasonal workers in achieving bargaining rights has already inspired similar movements in other states such as Texas and Florida. It has also put new strength back of the move to persuade Congress to extend collective bargaining rights and the benefits of the National Labor Relations Act to farm workers.

Clearly the collective bargaining route has been the most dependable road out of poverty for most American workers. There never has been, and still is, no *just* reason for continuing to deny it to workers in agriculture, particularly in the large, factory-in-the-field type of farm "industry."

HELP, INC., IN NEW MEXICO

> *How You and Your Family Look and Dress*
> *Food for You and Your Family*
> *Making Your Home More Useful and Attractive*
> *Understanding Yourself, Your Family and Friends*

—these subjects get high priority in the (H)elp, (E)ducation, (L)ivelihood (P)rogram of adult education for unemployed seasonal farm workers in New Mexico. Sponsored by the New Mexico Council of Churches and financed now with its third grant of funds from OEO, this project brings help and hope to deprived families in both northern and southern areas of the state.

Though family-centered, HELP is also community oriented, for it is trying to correct the tendency for the family emphasis, natural to Spanish-speaking people, to rule out "any true sense of community." The project, which operates through centrally located community education centers, hopes that participation will lead not only to better home environments and practices, but also to wider community interest, service and growth.

History and Development. All accounts of how HELP came to be give credit to more than 10 years of work and service by the United Church Women of New Mexico. When the New Mexico Council of Churches was organized in 1958 the Migrant Ministry, previously supported by UCW, became a department of the council.

Of particular interest to the ecumenically minded are the next stages in this historic development in which the council's Migrant Ministry (expanded into the Department of Cooperative Christian Concern) was joined by representatives of the Roman Catholic Archdiocese of Sante Fe as sponsors of an OEO meeting in Portales in mid-December 1964. Immediately following this meeting, the Roman Catholic Archdiocese of Sante Fe announced that it was joining the New Mexico Council of Churches—"*the first such act in the world.*" Thus what eventually emerged as HELP made history not only for the unemployed seasonal workers of New Mexico but for the whole world of religion through its unprecedented Roman Catholic–Protestant alliance.

"In April 1965 Governor Campbell requested the Council of Churches to sponsor a program for the state's underemployed seasonal agricultural workers," Rev. Harry Summers, Council of Churches executive, explained to me. A working meeting between OEO Migrant Branch representatives and interested individuals from northern and southern areas of the state then produced a statewide proposal, for which a grant of $1.36 million was approved on June 30, 1965.

Steps were quickly taken to start centers at Vado, Loving and Mora, and these were soon followed by 4 more at Roswell, Dexter, Hagerman and Lake Arthur. Somewhat later the number of centers were brought to 19 by locations throughout the Pecos Valley—Roswell, Rio Grande—Las Cruces, North Western—Espanola and North Eastern—Las Vegas sections. A second grant for $1.4 million approved in May 1965 made possible additional work in 3 of the most severely depressed counties of Mora, Taos and Sandoval, through which an additional 19 localities will be served.

How the Program Has Developed. How do you go about improving the home-education-livelihood prospects of families with deeply ingrained habits and attitudes, functional illiteracy often in 2 languages, and continuously decreasing economic resources and social adaptability to the rapidly changing community and world around them? HELP centers provide staff facilities for basic education, a foods laboratory, serving room, woodworking shop, day care center, food preparation galley, library, office and storage place. A shed for teaching welding and a rented garage for auto repairs may become part of the complex.

At HELP's central headquarters in Albuquerque, I spent some time with Mrs. Grace Miller, state education director, who supervises curriculum building and teacher training, particularly in homemaking.

123

She was then working on an improved set of teachers' guides. "When the mother's desire is for the bright new, ready-made dress she saw in the store window," said Mrs. Miller, "how do you induce her to remodel one that is much more available to her? How do you shift interest from a diet the family likes and is used to (however monotonous and low in nutrition) to one that will build the healthy, vigorous bodies so many need so badly?" Age-old questions, perhaps— but with countless new twists and turns, as new products, new methods, new knowledge of values and uses and persistently persuasive appeals to buy (where no means for buying exist) continue to complicate the problem day by day.

A bright side to the problem of finding qualified employees for the program has been the unexpectedly good performance of people recruited from the low-income groups as they were quickly trained in community development, center organization and some aspects of the educational programs. Effective use has also been made of VISTA volunteers, with 30 or more serving at various centers at one time.

Each community center is operated by a center committee of leaders from the group it serves. Interestingly, most of these committees opposed the use of training stipends. "This has been positive, rather than negative," said a central staffer, "because it established a certain integrity in the program that has prevented any assumptions by the public or participants that it is a 'give-away' or 'make-work' project." Even without this inducement the night classes on literacy had amazing participation, often from many who had been picking cotton all day. In one class of 59 adults, 47 had worked from sunup to sundown during the day.

While the HELP centers have been bringing a whole new dimension to the homes and education of thousands of New Mexico's most impoverished citizens, the directors feel the Center's greatest contribution is to livelihood as it becomes the "preparatory feeder" for job-centered programs developed by other agencies throughout the state.

The Churches' Role. The specific request by the governor to the New Mexico Council of Churches to draft and sponsor the HELP program gave official recognition to the long involvement of the council and many church people, both Protestant and Catholic, with the welfare of the agricultural migrants. While the council officially signed the first contract with OEO, it has since been replaced as contracting agent by a separately incorporated HELP Board of Trustees. Local churches and local migrant committees also were significantly involved in the early location of centers and recruitment of personnel.

A traumatic experience of potentially bitter proportions set in, therefore, when this obvious eagerness "to be of help where needed" on the part of church people met firm resistance from the staff and directors of HELP. Actually the situation in New Mexico was only an overt expression of a natural antagonism between "professionals" and would-be "helpers" which was evident in one form or another in several church-sponsored, professionally operated programs.

In the New Mexico situation a number of obstacles to volunteer participation soon became evident, over and above the often alleged "overeagerness without competence." The Centers were thought to have little effective place for "nonpoor" volunteers. Centers were physically located where the people who wanted to help were not. Volunteers often proved unreliable attendants at training sessions. Many program participants came from Spanish backgrounds with a primitive religion, producing a natural hostility to adherents of the traditional "mainline" religious establishment. Language differences have been a further handicap.

A good deal of second thinking has taken place on both sides of this prickly issue. Not only is a definite move on foot to encourage more participation from churches and church people, but specific suggestions are being followed. Important among these are: an effort to increase awareness among church people of the centers' need for professional help, including the possibility of part-time help, *for pay;* an effort to inform and enlist the active interest and help of the smaller churches located in the center areas (whose members are more likely to identify, in both language and culture, with the program participants); and commitment on the part of the staff to give concrete attention to points at which nonprofessionals can be used.

The church people are again hopeful of realizing much good for all concerned through a cooperative rather than a combative approach to the vast undertaking which still needs constructive contribution from every possible source.

ASSOCIATED MIGRANT OPPORTUNITY SERVICES, INC., OF INDIANA

Confronted with an annual influx of 20,000 Mexican-Americans, most of whom live in various stages of misery while they help to harvest the state's fruit and vegetable crops, church men and women of Indiana eagerly grasped the opportunity for help through the Economic Opportunity Act.

Representatives of the 26-year-old Indiana Council of Churches Migrant Ministry and the 16-year-old Migrant Apostolate of the Catholic Diocese of Indiana met in late summer 1964 to formulate plans for a statewide cooperative program. By February 1965 they were ready to move as a body to form the nonprofit corporation called Associated Migrant Opportunity Services, Inc. (AMOS), and shortly thereafter an OEO grant of $484,000 was approved for the first year's operation.

AMOS itself is the enabling, helping and supervisory agent. The program is carried out mainly through local, countywide migrant councils, providing maximum feasible participation of residents of the county, including one-third migrant representation.

As explained by Jon M. Templin, the state director, AMOS during its first year organized 15 program components, with an overwhelming emphasis on children and youth education. They included: 5 remedial schools to help disadvantaged migrant youth of school age catch up with their settled peers; 3 day care centers to help preschool children prepare for school experience; a day camp which provided an educational opportunity for cooperative living for migrant youngsters; a cultural and social education program which gave migrant teenagers and young adults an opportunity to meet and share experiences with other Americans of like age; a literacy program designed to help migrants gain or improve English-language skills in speaking, reading and writing; an adult education program aimed at teaching the Spanish speaking migrant more facility in the use of English, along with citizenship training, money management, leadership and community aide work; 2 community centers which serve as focal points for migrant activities, services, information and referral; and the overall administrative unit designed to plan, organize, coordinate and supervise the total project. The programs reached 1,600 workers in 10 counties, including 1,150 children and youth under 20 years old. AMOS policy is to hire local residents "according to their availability and competence."

An unusual feature of AMOS has been its use of statewide groups or agencies to provide certain overall services to the local areas. For instance the Indiana State Council of Churches secured the services of Dr. William Briggs, a well-known educator, who with one assistant trained some 500 volunteers in techniques of literacy education. They in turn set up local training projects. Ball State University conducted the teacher training workshops.

On July 1, 1966 the program was funded for a second 15-month period. The grant of $865,000 provides 10 delegate agencies and 36 program components, with main attention turning from children to adults, and with special emphasis on helping migrant families who want to settle permanently in Indiana. A delegate agency in South Bend, *Centro Cristiano de la Comunidad* (Christian Community Center), has launched a training and placement project in cooperation with MDTA. Six county components are also planning to relate their activities to area vocational training schools and on-the-job training assignments. In October 1966, the project was helping to "settle" migrants at the rate of over 300 families during the year.

Successful adult education trainees are now making $4,000 or more a year. In fact AMOS now claims that the projected one-year income of persons trained in the last year will exceed the total cost of the adult education program of $220,000. While job training is coming to the forefront, stress is also continuing on basic and high school equivalency education. Permanent housing needs also loom large, and central staff and some local components are exploring the possibilities of installing mobile home units or developing self-help housing projects with the Farmers Home Administration. "What we need is a halfway kind of house," said a staff member. This is regarded as an ideal project for churches, "since the families need help only long enough to get started."

This newest and most promising of the many "programs for migrants" undertaken in Indiana over the years was started by the combined religious forces of the state. The first incorporators of AMOS were 6 Roman Catholic and 6 Protestant church leaders, and they have continued in that proportion on the board of directors. Rev. Grover C. Hartman, executive secretary of the Indiana Council of Churches, has been twice elected president. The secretary is Father Bates and the treasurer Father Doherty of the Catholic Archdiocese. Interreligious leadership also exists in the local migrant councils, for instance, in Grant County, where the official board has equal membership of Catholics, Protestants and Jews. Local ministers or priests are chairmen or vice chairmen of 5 of the 13 county migrant councils.

In carrying responsibility for the literacy training program, the Indiana State Council of Churches has involved hundreds of volunteers, who give time both to become trained and later to train others and to help with literacy programs in their home areas. Volunteers make up the delegate agency boards, and many local programs use volunteers in various capacities. In community education stress is laid on interrelationships between migrants and settled residents. Cultural programs bring all groups together, as in the Tri-County Social Education program with fiestas, dances and open-house gatherings.

INDIAN CENTERS AND SERVICES

At the time of my study there seemed to be few, if any, broad anti-poverty efforts on behalf of American Indians which approached in

127

scope the migrant farm-worker programs. I was able, however, to visit or learn about 2 city-centered projects exclusively of, by or for Indians to which the churches are related. They are the American Indian Center and St. Augustine's Center for American Indians, both located in Chicago.

AMERICAN INDIAN CENTER

Chicago has among its citizens over 10,000 American Indians. They have made their homes in all areas of Chicago, and no one neighborhood seems to be their own. But there is one place where all can meet to talk in familiar ways about family and friends, about problems, jobs and opportunities. This is at their own American Indian Center on the corner of Sheridan Road and Broadway.

Emphasis on "their own" is important, for the Center is wholly operated and up to 60 percent financially supported by its Indian membership. Indians of over 80 different tribes have been involved in its activities. Only Indians may vote in its elections, though its staff positions and membership in the Center itself are open to anyone interested and qualified.

All programs and policy decisions are determined by Center members acting through monthly meetings of its board and through ongoing activities of program and standing committees. "One of our central problems," said Robert W. Rietz, the Center director, "is how to communicate to newcomers that the Center is theirs and should represent their efforts and achievement." Difficult as it may be, the Center has done a fine job of translating its self-responsibility and self-help principles into a lively morning, noon and night program involving participation of over 5,000 persons served through its family services and through a fluctuating membership of around 2,600.

The Center's social activities for all ages rate high, the most popular being the weekly family night program attended by entire families from infants to grandparents. One night each month offers a get-acquainted supper followed by a "Pow Wow." Many activities are undertaken to raise funds for self-help financial support, which is an essential part of the Center's sense of independence and responsibility.

A second important activity is the family service program, staffed by one professional case worker with volunteer assistance, through which a constant flow of help, counseling and referral is maintained. Problems range from rehabilitation of skid row alcoholics to assistance with career training or sharing in a devastating family crisis. Attention is also given to job referrals and training opportunities and to complications of selling lands "back home," maintaining contacts with reservations and complying with laws which regulate many other aspects of an Indian's daily life and activities.

Increasing concern for the development and attitudes of school-age youngsters led in 1965 to the extension of the summer day camp activities into a fall and winter Explorer program, with stress on school work as "exploration of the world" and on building confidence that a rewarding career can really happen, for them, if started *"now."*

Where do the churches come in? Their main contact was at the beginning stage. The initial idea for the Center plus a contribution toward its launching came from the American Friends Service Committee. Interest and help were also provided by the Indian Ministry Committee of the Chicago Church Federation, by a staff member of the Chicago Baptist Association and of the Methodist Rock River Conference. With a maximum of encouragement and a minimum of financial help a small corps of Indian leaders picked up and carried the idea through its struggling early days and on to its emergence into the present Center. Though funds are no longer contributed directly from church sources, church-related staff and members continue an active personal interest in the Center and help in whatever practical ways are available in its program and fund-raising activities.

ST. AUGUSTINE'S CENTER FOR AMERICAN INDIANS

Primarily a social casework center, St. Augustine's provides services to Indians and their families coming to or resident in Chicago. The Center, organized in 1961 as a project of the Episcopal Diocese of Chicago and the Executive Council of the Episcopal Church, is located in an area estimated to include some 4,000 Indian families.

"Identification with the First Americans in every area of their needs and aspirations has long been our goal," said Peter J. Powell, the priest who is director of the Center. From its beginning St. Augustine's Center has provided family assistance and counseling, guided recreation, legal and medical aid, plus some financial means for supplementary education. Since July 1965 it has been able with the help of OEO funds to expand its programs.

One special emphasis is work with families where drinking is a major problem. Two psychiatric social workers carry responsibility for rehabilitative programs. The staff works with an advisory group of leaders in the Indian community who have themselves experienced difficulties with the drinking problem. The Center also works closely with the Montrose Urban Progress Center (an official OEO agency), referring families to its programs, services and job opportunities.

During 1965 the Center recorded interviews with 5,274 Indians and 634 non-Indians; 913 families and single individuals received its casework services. The Center is related to the 146 Episcopal parishes in the Chicago Diocese through its American Indian Work Council.

Continuing needs of the migrants are well summarized in an analysis by Jon M. Templin of AMOS. Though expressed in terms of his Indiana experience, the conclusions apply generally across the nation. He says in brief:

"Although many wonders have been worked and many doors opened for Indiana migrants, AMOS has only just begun to cope with the multiple and diversified migrant needs awaiting assistance. Among the major tasks awaiting the wholehearted efforts of an aroused and enlightened citizenry are the following: 1) elimination of child labor abuses; 2) elimination of residence requirements and service restrictions; 3) improved migrant housing conditions; 4) better media for transporting farm labor; 5) specialized assistance for the migrant who wants to settle out; 6) improvement and expansion of established services; 7) development of new and more comprehensive programs in answer to migrant needs; and 8) establishment of more adequate wage scales for farm labor in connection with the eventual goal of year-round, stabilized work.

"All these problem areas need immediate attention. But the presence and exploitation of child labor is, in my opinion, the most grievous sin. . . ."

Many people head their list of pressing farm labor needs with its nationwide inclusion under the National Labor Relations Act. This involves extending to workers on the nation's farms—particularly those farms now reaching "industry" size and employment needs—the same right enjoyed by other American workers to engage in collective bargaining with the same protection as other workers.[1]

On behalf of our American Indian population, much promise for those leaving the reservations in large numbers seems to lie in efforts typified by Chicago's American Indian Center. These go beyond the necessary but ever-recurring extension of welfare services to the building of a firm, self-help "power structure" capable of understanding, developing and advancing a program "of their own." If this desirable end is to be achieved much more help by the larger community, particularly the religious community, is urgently needed.

---

[1] In November 1966, a 7-state Mid-West Conference for OEO-sponsored Migrant Programs (initiated by AMOS) made extension of National Labor Relations Act coverage to migrant workers its number one resolution.

10 A New Breed of Volunteers

"We need a new breed of volunteer to be our interpreters," Mrs. Peggy Ann Way, Social Welfare Consultant of the Chicago City Missionary Society told the National Presbyterian Health and Welfare Association at its Biennial Conference in January 1965.

"That is assuming, of course, the other half of the story: that we are developing a new breed of services, a new depth of mission, a contemporary sense of priority, more flexible structures, more profound views of the nature of persons and society." Only because of their ability to involve large numbers of volunteers with this "new" approach and spirit have many church-related anti-poverty programs been able to start at all or continue beyond the first, faltering stages.

What is so new about them? Here, in condensed version, is Mrs. Way's formula:

First, this new breed of volunteer must combine involvement in services with involvement in attacking the roots of social problems that make such services necessary. A ministry with persons must be held in clear tension with a ministry with (social and political) institutions.

Second, this new volunteer must be actively involved in the urgent issues of our time and in the lives of the persons whom they affect. Involvement means knowledge; involvement means direct experience; *involvement means investment of self, and let us no longer pretend it does not.*

Third, the involvement must be done out of a perspective of mutuality. The volunteer comes to share in the common problems of humanity, the mutual concerns of citizens. He is no longer a philanthropist, but a participant.

Fourth, this new breed of volunteer is prepared to engage in direct action or protest, when his own conscience drives him to do so. At the very least, he does not immediately react negatively when direct action is anticipated, discussed or realized.

Fifth, our new volunteer is reflective. He probes into the difficult tension between the provision of services and the changing of the social order. He is self-conscious about priorities. *He is not hard-headed, but he is realistic.*

Sixth, our new breed participates in the creation of new structures as they are called forth by the needs of contemporary man. He is willing to experiment, both within present structures and in the creation of new ones.

This new kind of helper and help first came into prominence through the direct involvement programs of the student movements of the past decade. This outpouring of self on the part of students came to sharpest focus in the civil rights movement; it has continued, less spectacularly but steadfastly, in poverty war programs.

Women, too—the age-long bulwark of volunteer giving for others—are swelling the ranks of the new volunteer. This is happening, first, as many from an earlier day have been able to enlarge their vision to add issues to services, to accept involvement of self as well as substance, and to encourage creation of new structures and services; it is happening also, as Mrs. Way points out, as "the new generation of college educated suburban (and other) wives look for ways to make use of their skills and their persons"; and further as "the growing number of middle class Negro(s) are becoming increasingly involved in the plight of the slum situations from which many of them have only recently emerged." To this list of helpers available to poverty programs I would add, as the most "realistic" of all, the mothers and other women living in poverty themselves who are giving volunteer services.

With more leisure time and the down-to-earth appeal of many antipoverty projects, more and more men are also volunteering to help under the "new breed" approach.

Expressed in the concrete terms of a church-related, child-parent program, the "new" requirements are spelled out in a job description for volunteers in the prospectus for "Project Uplift" at Southminster Presbyterian Church in Phoenix, Arizona. A good poverty project model, it provides that among personal qualifications a volunteer must have good health and emotional stability, ability to exercise patience and establish warm relationships with children "who are different," interest in and respect for people of all groups, understanding of children through practical experience as a parent or as a participant in community groups, willingness to train for the program, to give regular and dependable service and to wear appropriate dress that will not set the volunteer apart from those he or she is working with.

STUDENT CONTRIBUTIONS

Most of my trips were made during the summer, when students—college and/or high school—were giving their energy and enthusiasm to practically every project.

Year-round help from students is also increasing, for example, as schools of social work assign graduate students for field service. Seminaries, too, have discovered the poverty areas and programs (often crowding their doorsteps) as points for service and experience. Blocks of time are also volunteered by students including high schoolers, in tutoring programs "in every part of the country and in almost every imaginable sort of community." Peter Schrag, rating the volunteer tutorial programs as "the most powerful force for educational reform on the American scene today," gives most credit to college and high school students who "go to the slums of the inner city, to a rural church, or to a local welfare center . . . helping a child through his arithmetic or his reading." He further notes that high school students being tutored by college undergraduates are in turn often tutoring youngsters in the elementary schools. Again, the gain realized by the tutors, in satisfaction to conscience and even in learning about learning, frequently equals or exceeds the help to those being tutored.

Volunteer student programs have been much discussed and written about. Student work has been considered in this study only as one of the many phases of the anti-poverty effort. Described are two projects that depend almost entirely on students.

PARKWAY HOUSE PARISH, HOUSTON, TEXAS

Rev. Jimmie A. Reese, Minister to Parkway House Parish in Houston, supported by the Methodist Conference in a section with a 1,000-apartment public housing unit and an all-Negro population, operates a varied program of outreach to its youth. These activities are made possible through the help of young conscientious objectors from the Church of the Brethren assigned to work in this difficult area through the Protestant Charities of Houston.

Major features of this program for youth are "Breakout" and "Tree House." "Breakout is an outgrowth of our feelings of frustration over the traditional recreation-social program for teen-agers," said Mr. Reese. It represents an attempt, after several months of conversations between the student staff and the teen-agers, to give the young people

133

an experience outside the housing project area, with a cross-section of their peers of various economic levels.

Tree House is a coffee house, "not unique when you look at the national picture, but quite unique when you look at the Houston picture." With spontaneous group singing, "certain kinds of readings" and short movies aimed at producing immediate response, the staff are getting to know the young people in the Negro slum area.

A successful 8-week Student Workshop on Social Welfare and Poverty, conducted in summer 1965 for senior high school students, led to its expansion in 1966 to include college as well as high school students from Texas and other states. Another group of Church of the Brethren students joined the project for the summer months.

YOUTH ACTIVITY PROGRAM, DAYTON, OHIO

Rev. Ivan G. Kurtz, pastor of Pleasant Valley United Church of Christ, directs a community-centered program sponsored by his congregation and staffed by one seminary student, employed part-time by funds from the Church's Youth Activity Committee, 3 volunteer students from nearby United Theological Seminary (EUB) and volunteer women and students from St. Mark's Episcopal, Good Shepherd EUB and Pleasant Valley UCC churches.

Most of the programs are designed for children and youth, though recent expansion has included adults from the neighborhood. Activities center in the church itself or in a renovated barn known as the Mobile Court Mission, serving a densely populated area of permanently parked mobile homes.

Year-round programs include recreation for children and youth; opportunities "to grow in social and cultural relations with one another, the community and the world"; contacts that open doors to dealing with emotional problems; opportunities for the total community, both mobile residents and stationary "home folks," to relate to one another in an integrated community; and provision of an agency through which problems of the community can be recognized and met through its many resources. The program is seeking wider interchurch and community involvement and support through broadening the representation on its advisory board of local civic groups, the school system, mobile court managers and residents.

WOMEN, MEN AND THE JOB CORPS

Traditionally, in the churches and now in the poverty war, women provide the volunteer back-up which alone makes many projects possible. Men, with less day time at their disposal and hence not looked to earlier for volunteer help in quantity, are also now enlisting more and more frequently for volunteer services.

WOMEN IN COMMUNITY SERVICE (WICS)

The most dramatic contribution of volunteer service to the poverty war to date has been made through WICS—Women in Community Service. WICS is an incorporated agency formed by 4 national women's organizations: the National Council of Catholic Women, National Council of Jewish Women, National Council of Negro Women and United Church Women of the National Council of Churches. It is set up to recruit and screen girls from 16 to 21 for the women's Job Corps Training Centers.

Under its contract with OEO, WICS has set up 150 recruitment centers across the country. With only volunteer directors and staffs in each Center, local members of the 4 contracting organizations enlisted during 1966 more than 10,000 volunteers. These volunteer workers then visited, counseled and worked with the families of some 60,000 girls who were screened for inclusion in 12 women's Job Corps Centers. From this number 13,000 were referred as acceptable applicants under Job Corps regulations.

The women recruiters keep in touch with their trainees who are accepted, through letters and other supportive services to the girls and their families. The girls who are not accepted for Job Corps training, as well as many not even eligible for screening, have been helped with personal counseling, referral to other sources of guidance or in other ways.

WICS' efforts have proved so successful that OEO has encouraged the women to broaden their activities, under its Community Action Programs, to bring still other forms of help to girls of this age group, both those now beginning to return from the Job Corps Centers and those not able to go. As this is being written, 21 proposals for this expanded activity are in various stages of processing. Confronted first with delayed action by Congress and finally by curtailed funds for CAP programs, OEO had approved only 2 supplementary grants up to February 1967. These were made to WICS groups in *Miami, Florida* ($17,000 for a program of referral and follow-through, remedial education and self-improvement, dental and psychiatric care, limited vocational training and assistance in job placement) and *Salem, Oregon* ($9,000 for a counseling center and clearing house, general education development courses and training in practical nursing).

At *Richmond, Virginia,* "we became discouraged waiting for our supplementary grant to be approved," said Mrs. Dorothy Lasday, WICS director, "so we have gone ahead with what resources we have." They have specialized in a program to prepare the girls, accepted (or pending acceptance) for the Job Corps, for the new experiences ahead of them. The program, "Orientation to the world of work—and the Job Corps," involves classes in physical fitness, grooming and care of clothing; tours to the state capitol, the Federal Reserve Bank and a local factory employing a large number of women; experiences in interracial group living; visits with a nutrition specialist to neighborhood food shops and supermarkets for techniques of wise buying and comparison shopping.

"These girls have lived a monochromatic existence," said Mrs. Lasday, "and they are thrown by any new experience. We feel the shock is easier to take here at home than at a Job Corps Center many miles from familiar territory." The Richmond Center is also beginning follow-up work with Job Corps returnees coming back to their home communities.

Robert Young, Assistant Director of the Job Corps, calls WICS "a fantastically varied group of women. They are an illogical organization . . . not experienced in this type of work . . . volunteers . . . all things that experienced organizations traditionally avoid. But they have one great attribute—they are overwhelmingly successful."

JOINT ACTION IN COMMUNITY SERVICE, INC. (JACS)

JACS is a new nonprofit organization working in cooperation with WICS to help Job Corps returnees to find jobs and to adjust to the community and the job.

Formed by a group of men closely associated with the National Council of Churches, the National Catholic Community Service and the National Conference of Catholic Charities, JACS board of directors will include representatives of a wide range of community service agencies.

An initial OEO grant of $214,500, announced in late January 1967, is expected to provide directorship services for programs related to OEO's 7 regional offices and for those in several other larger metropolitan centers. Local volunteers will be enlisted for the contact work with the Corps returnees. In cooperation with local Employment Service offices, JACS workers "will direct these young people to employment channels and make sure that employment assistance is provided until a satisfactory job adjustment is made." The help may also include locating a place to live, determining means of transportation to the job (a major hurdle in many localities), providing financial guidance and introduction into community and social activities.

136

LOCAL CHURCH RELATIONS TO JOB CORPS
CENTERS AND TRAINEES

During the course of this study I encountered one concerted, church-related outreach to a men's Job Corps Center that went beyond the customary "invitation to attend church services." This program, related to the Breckenridge Job Corps Center in Indiana, has been developed by the Job Corps Committee of the Greater Evansville Association of Clergymen involving all three faiths.

Much of the Evansville church program is related to the Evansville Job Corps Recreation Center located in the downtown area, and involves the downtown churches. In a letter to their clergy brothers the Committee suggested 4 ways the churches could be of service to Job Corpsmen at Breckenridge: 1) opening worship services to Corpsmen and providing transportation from the Evansville Center to the church; 2) sending a youth (or other) group to Breckenridge for a tour of facilities; 3) having youth fellowship groups visit the recreation center in Evansville "to get to know the Corpsmen better"; and 4) encouraging parishioners to invite Corpsmen to their homes for dinner and relaxation on Sunday.

"We are emphasizing home visitation and local groups touring the Corps facilities and this is working fairly well," said Rev. Philip Hoy, chairman of the Job Corps Committee.

Ministerial associations in Evansville and neighboring Henderson, Morganfield and Sturgis, Kentucky, joined in getting the Center to add a religious coordinator to its staff. In this capacity Rev. Gerald Stone, a Presbyterian with experience in inner-city work, has formed an advisory council of ministers and included 2 Corpsmen. "This," said Mr. Hoy, "has facilitated communications among all groups."

Local church relations with women's Job Corps Centers are usually developed through the United Church Women. Representative is the Roman Catholic–Protestant program recently set up in Cleveland, Ohio, where arrangements have been made to have the Center girls indicate what religious group, if any, they would like to have contact with. Around 25 (of the 300) girls have elected to take this opportunity, though the number went as high as 65 during Christmas.

A host family picks the girls up at the Center on Sunday, taking them to church and then to their homes for the rest of the day. Catholic families carry out this program each week; Protestants once a month, rotating the program among denominations.

137

A more comprehensive program has been planned in connection with the new Keystone Job Corps Center for Women near Hazleton, Pennsylvania, where the Center's opening meant that "450 girls who are poor, culturally and socially deprived, school drop-outs, many of whom will be Negro, plus 170 staff persons (also white and Negro) augmented the population of the Hazleton–Butler Valley area of Pennsylvania."

Representatives of the women's groups of the area, including three Councils of United Church Women, came together around the need to prepare the residents of the whole section (where there are now no resident Negroes) to receive this new group of people "in happy and meaningful relationships in community and into the life and mission of the churches." A local unit of WICS has been formed and efforts are being made to enlist the churches and community groups in an understanding outreach to the Corps women and staff.

PROGRAMS FOR THE AGING IN POVERTY

Practically every church or council of churches has a program involving older members of the church or community. Frequently these include a visiting, and sometimes a home service, component staffed by a corps of volunteers. In my travels, however, I found practically no church-related programs designed especially to reach old people living in poverty areas where, of all the miserable people, the old and infirm are invariably the most miserable. One inspiring exception to this neglect of the elderly poor is described here.

SELF-HELP SERVICES FOR THE ELDERLY, SAN FRANCISCO, CALIFORNIA

"Some of the stories that seniors in the poverty area tell us are so incredible it makes them sound paranoid," said Mrs. Milton Schiffman, Council of Churches' Planner on Aging. Yet investigation often proves the tales to be all too true. She cited the story of Mrs. P., an 80-year-old lady living in a dilapidated tenement in the North Beach–Chinatown area. Mrs. P. kept complaining that people were walking through her apartment and she couldn't lock her door. When, after repeated complaints, the Friendly Visitor finally went home with Mrs. P., she found the landlord, making some forced repairs on a rickety front stairway, had put cement in Mrs. P.'s lock and told inhabitants of the upper floors just to go through her apartment—the only access to the previously abandoned back stair well.

Many experiences such as this or worse were encountered during a volunteer Friendly Visitor program pioneered for some years in 15 local neighborhoods through member churches of the San Francisco Council of Churches, under Mrs. Schiffman's leadership. The success of this program led the Ford Foundation to underwrite a special project, using the Council of Churches techniques and volunteer personnel, as one part of a nationwide study of the elderly in urban renewal.

The study evaluation concluded that *a trusted personal counselor* to put the elderly in touch with the services they need is the vital missing link in most established welfare programs for old people. Most significant of the study's conclusions from the anti-poverty angle was recognition that the council's program "succeeded nobly" largely because its volunteer workers possessed both the "selflessness and time" required to establish a trusting relationship with the old people they sought to serve.

Acting on this impressive endorsement of her volunteer visitor approach, Mrs. Schiffman, with continued backing of the Council of Churches, has received OEO funding for a comprehensive Friendly Visitor program in the city's blighted Chinatown—North Beach District, called "Self-Help Services for the Elderly."

Through 14 Friendly Visitor aides, drawn as far as possible from persons 50 years or older from the area, will be funneled the basic services for which the recipients would normally have to go to many different places and agencies. After a 6-week training course the aides maintain contact with the elderly residents, learn about their gripes and pains, spread basic health information, act as agents for the special "self-help services," including help with homemaking, with moving, relocation, health care, and even catering services and portable meals.

A centrally located Drop-In Center houses offices of the contact and housing staffs and provides a rallying point for the entire program. Mrs. Schiffman, the supervising coordinator, with her assistant, is responsible for promoting the overall purpose of the project: "to interest the elderly so they become ready to make an investment in living, to improve their financial, social and moral standing in the community."[1]

Greater opportunities for programs for older people are now available under the new Older Americans Act adopted by the 89th Congress (P.L. 89-73). More, many more, projects directed to the needs of the elderly poor should be sponsored by church groups.

[1] This project has been funded by OEO for a second time, and there has been a new grant for a similar program in the Tenderloin—Skid Row area of San Francisco.

CHURCH-SPONSORED TRAINING PROGRAMS FOR VOLUNTEERS

CITY MISSIONARY SOCIETY PROGRAM, CHICAGO, ILLINOIS

Mrs. Peggy Ann Way, Chicago City Missionary Society consultant, who cited the need for the "new breed" in church-related volunteer services, is herself deeply involved in helping to produce them. The newest approach to training in the society's traditional volunteer-registry department is called a Training Program in Metropolitan Lay Ministry. The Presbytery and Episcopal Diocese of Chicago have joined the Missionary Society in sponsoring it.

Training sessions are conducted on 4 consecutive mornings or evenings in 4 sections of the city. The course's appeal and strength lie in combining orientation, confrontation, training and involvement in one brief span. Over 300 persons have sought involvement in the program, coming from Methodist, Lutheran, Roman Catholic, Presbyterian, Episcopal and United Church of Christ churches.

Through emphasis on the new and broader view of the role of church lay men, women and youth, the program seeks "to change the focus of the church from institution to mission." It sees the church as a "home base" and a "power house" from which members "venture forth to bridge ethnic, class and racial barriers which divide the world."

VOLUNTEER RECRUITMENT AND TRAINING
IN MINNEAPOLIS CHURCHES

Rev. Helen G. M. Galazka, director of Christian Social Relations and United Church Women in the Greater Minneapolis Council of Churches, has in operation an effective process for enlisting and orienting lay men and women of both city and suburban churches in her "greater" area. It acts as a clearing house through which needs and volunteers are related, circulates a regular bulletin with this kind of information and holds monthly orientation meetings to which potential volunteers are invited.

The monthly all-day sessions involve a changing group of people from various areas. Following a talk or film on the inner-city situation in Minneapolis, "the experts" describe successes and failures of programs, pastors tell where they see needs and Mrs. Galazka outlines what other cities are doing. The group then divides into workshops, concentrating on special interest areas such as youth programming, visitation of the aging, work with people in poverty or contacts with minorities.

"We have had help from AFDC mothers, and minority group representatives add their own points of view," said Mrs. Galazka. When the trainees come from suburban churches they are taken on tours of the inner city, stopping at a public school, day care center and settlement house. The group then returns to the Center for discussion of what they have seen and what can be done. This is followed at a later date by a training session in their own church, with emphasis on the area in which they decide to work.

Indication of the many kinds of services that can be volunteered in this representative city of many needs comes from the monthly "opportunities" bulletin. A recent one noted:

"Sister Church" relationships (in which a suburban church supplies leadership and/or support where the inner-city church has special needs) between Good Samaritan Methodist and Simpson Methodist; Christ Presbyterian and House of Faith Presbyterian; Westwood Lutheran and Prince of Glory Lutheran Churches.

Nursery School help from Peace Presbyterian to All Saints Episcopal; from St. Stephen's Episcopal to Community Covenant; St. Luke Presbyterian to Zion Baptist.

Day Care Center—"an outstanding example is Fifth Avenue Congregational Church."

Reading Enrichment and Tutoring Programs at Grace Presbyterian, Lake Nakomis Presbyterian and Simpson Methodist Churches, also Faith Mennonite (working with Pillsbury Citizens Service), Waite Neighborhood House, Simpson Methodist and Salem Covenant churches.

Youth Centers at Bethlehem Presbyterian (an all-age program), Highland Park Presbyterian (club night for neighborhood youth), Salem Covenant (cultural programs aimed at the "less chance child"), Wesley Methodist (coffee house for young adults), St. Peter's Lutheran and Messiah Lutheran (drop-in centers for teens), Community Church of the Brethren (Work Camp at Selby/Dale Area in St. Paul providing work for teens or young adults with mentally retarded children.)

I would be less than honest to leave the impression that all relationships are rosy between professional, paid workers and volunteer workers in anti-poverty activities.

While few situations of misunderstanding have developed into open antagonism as in the New Mexico HELP program (Chapter 9), I was aware, in a number of cases, of either an armed truce or state of strategic "noninvolvement" between project directors and the "horde of do-gooders" which at least one director seemed to think were threatening him.

Fortunately, however, in most instances where the use of volunteers had been initially resisted, I found that the current attitude had either changed completely or showed distinct signs of mellowing. The causes of the change have been the substantial and dependable help supplied by "volunteer" parents and others in the poverty areas themselves, and the readiness of many of the "new type" of volunteer to give understanding and reliable help when the opportunity has presented itself. To these I would add the increasing efforts of the growing number of "bridge-builders," such as Mrs. Way and Mrs. Galazka, with their special programs of enlistment and training.

As of this writing it is clear that "wised-up" administrators and "stirred-up" new breed volunteers are getting together in growing numbers and in effective ways that greatly strengthen the whole poverty war effort and its indispensable person-to-person activities.

11 How the Churches Have Functioned
some general observations

The president of East Oakland Parish reported to his board of directors at year end 1965 that "many things were going on, with people going off in all directions . . . but," he added, "this was a part of growth."

When you consider where the churches stood when the anti-poverty effort began in earnest in mid-1964, growth is the most evident phenomenon. Though well aware of the danger, as one man put it, of "too much exposure to the little that *is* happening in the Church today and too little exposure to the immensity of what is not," I am still convinced that what has been started and accomplished by church-related groups in the struggle against poverty in this brief initiating period of the anti-poverty war is vast in significance and contagious in its example of what can and hopefully will be done in the long pull that lies ahead.

WHY AND HOW ARE THE CHURCHES CONCERNED?

Amazingly, this question is still asked. The weighty theological debate goes on in solemn assemblies, seminaries and religious journals. More pertinent at the level of day-to-day involvement are answers given by those engaged in the process whose roots are in the church.

Back in the early days Dr. Cameron P. Hall, convener of the churchmen's 1962 exploratory consultation on "persistent poverty" and organizer of the National Council of Churches' Anti-Poverty Task Force, said: "If the Church is to carry out Christ's mission in today's world, *it must set its sights to no lesser task than helping to create the will in the American people to make poverty a thing of the past, as slavery now is.*"

Rev. Paul A. Younger, director of Cleveland's Protestant Ministry to Poverty, says:

"If the Church's role in the 'war on poverty' is truly a sign of God's presence in our day, then *to be faithful to her Lord, the Church must participate in the battle after the manner of her Lord, as servant.*"

In his "inciting" booklet, "Stop Pussyfooting Through a Revolution," Rev. J. Archie Hargraves says:

"The present pattern of our Christian churches . . . must be reversed. We must stop escaping involvement . . . stop running away. . . . *We must put on the whole armor of God and plunge bravely into a revolutionary style of life.*"

As Rev. Louis Huber, Director of St. Louis' Fellowship Center, expresses it:

"You and I were used to receiving love and attention from our parents. But this would be a luxury to most of the boys and girls who come here. A child has to be 'given to' before he can give anything back to society . . . *Somewhere along the line an investment has to be made in people as people.*"[1]

STEPS IN ORGANIZING AND OPERATING LOCAL PROJECTS

Fortunately, concerned people and groups also ask what more needs to be done and how to go about doing it. The specifics of both "what" and "how" are spelled out in detail in the foregoing chapters. Some general observations emerging from the study include: 1) considerations about where to begin (deciding where and how to "invest"), 2) whom to work with (developing allies), 3) problems of support and personnel (building financial support and staff), and 4) the attitudes of people both in poverty and in the pews (changing attitudes).

Deciding Where and How to "Invest." Some activities, such as education, child care and family renewal, seem to come most naturally within the church-connected orbit. In each of these fields church groups have organized or helped to organize projects covering a whole section of a state (as in CDGM in Mississippi), a whole city (as in Rochester's family renewal program), an immediate church neighborhood (as in the many single-congregation tutoring, Head Start or family-adoption activities). In each of these areas church groups or people also launched out early into untried fields, of which the Newark Pre-School program (predating Head Start), Literacy Volunteers

---

[1] Sources, for the quotations respectively: Report of Consultation of the Churches and Persistent Pockets of Poverty, National Council of Churches, 1962; *Signs of the City* (Inner City Protestant Parish, Cleveland) Winter 1964; publication of the Stewardship Council, United Church of Christ, 1963; *St. Louis Post Dispatch,* August 31, 1961.

of Syracuse, FLOC in Washington, D. C. and Detroit's Riverside Inner-City Parish are notable examples.

Some of the most significant church-sponsored programs have been in the economic fields of: job training and placement (as in OIC and AMOS); economic development at the community level (as in Yukon, Pa., Greenwood, S. D. and the Appalachian communities); broader, whole-area development (as in southern Ohio and Missouri's Bootheel); also in promotion of cooperatives and credit unions (operated most successfully by Roman Catholic groups in many communities).

Church groups have "invested" in lively, tough, but surprisingly durable new approaches to various forms of organization—group, union and community, such as ECCO, F.I.G.H.T., WSO, the California Migrant Ministry and St. Louis' Mid-City Community Congress.

Many church-connected, mid-city settlement houses, rural settlements and children's homes had long been "on location" when the poverty war began. They have continued their programs, though in many cases with changes of outlook and outreach called for by the new attack on poverty. As described in Chapter 7, this change has involved a shift from inward-directed to outward-directed programs to take the projects beyond the centers and into the neighborhoods, which often include massive housing developments.

Where a church group found or still finds itself searching for the best way to come into the war it has been necessary, and still is, to search out *first* what most needs to be done in the community or neighborhood, and *second* how the need can best be met. In most communities one or more responsible bodies have now made such a search and catalogued the basic needs. This body is usually an OEO board or advisory council, or for church-related groups it can be a city, county or state council of churches.

Difference of opinion has developed among poverty war "professionals," particularly in church projects, about the relative importance of "service" versus "organization" as the primary means of attacking poverty.

If one takes as a definition of "services" those processes that deal directly with individual persons, their goal may be seen as the building up of people (sometimes called human resource development). Such services include restoring or maintaining health, providing more adequate education, aiding families in numerous ways; and they aim ultimately at the restoration of self-respect and human dignity, the two most devastating casualties of poverty.

"Community organization" seeks to bring the victims of poverty together into cohesive groups—block, neighborhood, or community—to de-

145

cide democratically on the needs not being met or changes called for that can only be obtained from outside the area. As such groups make their combined influence felt at the "seats of power" and get tangible action for the whole group or community, the needs met or changes effected (stepped-up building code enforcement, improved police protection or attitudes, more adequate garbage collection, improved transportation facilities) also attack the broader, environmental causes of poverty not reached by "welfare" services.

Considering the need for both services and organization, it is difficult to see why an either/or choice is necessary. Concentration on either one alone, or on combining them, appears valid, depending on the attendant needs and circumstances. For instance, Literacy Volunteers of Syracuse fulfills a greatly needed service function, independent of any attempt at organization. The Mid-City Community Congress in St. Louis is a broadly based community organization, aimed at obtaining changes and influencing economic and social development for an entire area. Westminster Neighborhood Association in Watts combines services to individuals with work with block clubs and neighborhood councils.

The first-order importance of organization for effective community action is increasingly recognized by poverty project directors. Not only are some new groups (such as the MCCC in St. Louis) being formed; but staffs of service organizations and community centers are being augmented with group, neighborhood and community organizers. This trend is shown in projects as widely varied as the Pre-School Council of Newark, N.J. and the HELP farm worker program in New Mexico.

Most advocates of "organization" as a high priority for church groups cite the churches' advantage as relatively "free and independent" agencies in economics and politics. Organizing any group to function in the political arena invites controversy. "The dilemma," says Kenneth Waterman, "is that a genuine, free and effective political instrument of the poor cannot be granted by EOA or any other public program. It will be up to churches, foundations and other private institutions and organizations to provide 'seed money' for the poor to build their own effective organization."

Rev. David Barry, Executive Director of the New York City Mission Society, challenges church groups even more directly. "The churches," he says, "may find appropriate points at which to qualify as service agencies using anti-poverty funds, but . . . too much involvement of this kind can tempt us to play down our most important role, which is not to provide *services* to the poor, but to be *advocates* for the poor."

As political repercussions arise to discourage organizing poverty

146

area residents through the direct use of public funds, more religious leaders are accepting the validity of this need for private-source sponsorship. Not all suppliers of church funds or influence, however, necessarily encourage such entry into the "organization" fray. As Dr. Carothers says, troubles develop here, too, as "Methodists who want things changed run up against Methodists who would like things to be different without being changed."[2] But, he continues, "change we must, if different we would be;" and this I think represents the general consensus of the project directors visited.

Developing Allies. The projects studied have demonstrated practically every known combination of intergroup relations and sponsorship, often forming the backbone of the new order of activity I have called the anti-poverty "mix." This selection of partners represents an important second step by any beginning group as they ask themselves, how or with whom do we start working on the need?

It takes only a little looking around to find whether groups already working at a given problem would like additional help; whether there are groups that would be glad to help if the church group would start the ball rolling; or whether the new group should start on its own, with the hope—as usually happens—that helpers will soon appear. Encouraging here are the many projects (like Dort-Oak Park Neighborhood House in Flint, Mich. and Grace House in Richmond, Va.) in which one local congregation or even one small group has started a program and then been joined by one or more others, frequently ending as a neighborhood or community-wide activity.

On a broader scale are the experiences, such as the one leading to the St. Louis Mid-City Congress, in which several ministers in an area found that each one was struggling with problems of a deteriorating neighborhood far too heavy to carry alone. Many difficulties are already yielding to concerted attack now that the possibility has been recognized. These cooperative ventures have frequently been started or advanced through a local council of churches or smaller-area ministers' group, often attracting the cooperation of Roman Catholic and Jewish groups as well. A denomination, taking the lead in organizing its churches within a diocese or synod, as in the Missouri Delta Ecumenical Ministry, is almost certain to be joined later by other churches.

Local congregations have become anti-poverty involved by being asked to contribute facilities for preschool, Head Start, tutoring and/or adult education programs. These arrangements may or may not in-

[2] *Keepers of the Poor*, Methodist Board of Missions, 1966, p. 125.

volve the congregation beyond the provision of unused space and payment for utilities. But even this seemingly simple arrangement has required numerous local congregations to face the fact that their church school or other facilities fail to meet official safety and sanitation standards. Surprised, stunned or just "hurt," boards of trustees have usually moved quickly to correct the unsafe conditions called to their attention; others have backed away "sorrowfully" from further efforts to house poverty war projects.

Not widely realized is the fact that, when all the churches are added up across the land, they clearly have more weekday unused space at their disposal than any other institutions, public or private, in the nation. These facilities, furthermore, are located "where the people are," at the heart of every inner-city neighborhood, village square or rural crossroads. Churches, too, own hospitals, homes, apartment houses and other usable properties in large numbers. As shown on every page of this book, many of these facilities have already been put into service; obviously many times the present number could and should be so used. With transportation now available through use of rented or volunteered buses or cars, even the spacious accommodations of churches in affluent outer-city or suburban areas can be put to good use.

Two basic "ingredients" seem essential to generating a church-related anti-poverty project. 1) Almost without exception a local project begins in the mind and through the driving force of *one individual* or *very small group of individuals* who are able to "leaven the lump" of the larger congregation and organize a sponsoring nucleus. 2) If there is then available to this small nucleus an *already functioning larger body*, such as a council of churches or denominational conference, synod or diocesan office, to which the smaller group can turn for guidance or perhaps financial support, the small group can then get "into orbit."

Building Financial Support and Staff. Besides releasing the growing eagerness of many Americans to "do something about poverty," Congress's main contribution in launching the poverty war was to provide, for the first time, money with which to start an across the country attack. In providing further that, within proper guidelines, the funds could be used by private as well as public agencies, wide participation by social, educational and religious groups was made possible.

This development immediately highlighted for religious groups the church-state issue, particularly as it relates to provision of "social services." While the philosophical debate on this issue has continued, many church groups have gone forward with their projects, making whatever financial arrangements their particular situation, plans and accessible resources called for. The result adds up to a variety of financing patterns almost as numerous as the structural and partnership patterns. One notable factor is the apparent absence of any blanket, from-the-top prohibition against the use of public funds, where deemed necessary, in the local church-related projects.

Among the groups visited some have followed the pattern set early by the Newark Pre-School Council, Inc., in which the parties contracting with the federal government were individuals acting in their own right. In Newark the religious and other nongovernmental agencies are informally "represented" through members at large on the Pre-School Council's board of directors. Numerous other related groups, after the pattern of the Council of Churches of Greater Cleveland, the New Mexico and Indiana Councils of Churches (joined by Roman Catholic groups) and Southminster Presbyterian Church in Phoenix, Arizona, have contracted directly (or through a church-responsible contracting board) for grants from one or more federal agencies.

Many projects are financed by a combination of private (usually church-based) and public (usually but not exclusively federal) funds. Their institutional facilities, core operating staffs and some parts of the programs are church-financed. Specific service components, such as Head Start and adult education, and frequently their community organization activities, are covered by public fund grants. Examples here include most of the comprehensive community center programs like Fellowship in St. Louis, Westminster in Watts and Susannah Wesley in Honolulu. These private-public programs sometimes also receive local community fund grants and occasionally state and/or city funds.

Surprising, to me at least, is the extent to which numerous church-related anti-poverty programs function without the aid of any public money. These projects are supported by church funds, supplemented occasionally by other private sources, such as foundations, neighborhood, business and labor groups. Examples from the study include Rochester's F.I.G.H.T., Portland's C-CAP, California Migrant Ministry, FLOC, Inc. in Washington, all of the programs related to welfare recipients and many local, single-congregation or single-denomination projects.

In some church-supported projects community organization for action on public issues (controversial or even militant, if necessary) is their main activity. This would seem to support the view that independently financed church groups are better able to serve as "advocates" of the poor or to lead them to become their own advocates, than groups "hampered" by accepting public funds. An indication that

149

the federal government welcomes partnership with religious groups in fostering self-help, "speaking-up" community activity, is shown, however, in the many instances in which church-related projects use federal funds specifically for block club, neighborhood and community organizing. This is increasingly emphasized in community centers and in the farm labor programs, where it is frequently assigned to provide VISTA workers.

Church financing of church-related projects is helped materially by the built-in endowment churches have of two of the war's most expensive features—physical facilities and personnel. Factors relating to facilities have been discussed. Regarding personnel, two things should be stressed again under financial assets. To begin with church-reared and trained "professionals" who have elected to work in the anti-poverty field, while reasonably well paid, are certainly not in anti-poverty work for its financial return. This fact can amount to a sizable item in holding down the overall cost of churches' poverty-project financing. The "new breed" volunteers are a second important budget-relieving source.

In terms of the operators here described and the church leaders who support them, the record indicated prevalence of a flexible rather than a doctrinaire approach to church-state relationships. The fact that some projects are now operating with their third public grants could indicate, as some fear, that they have succumbed to the government lure and know how to "crawl hat in hand" to Washington. It could indicate, on the other hand, a growing partnership of mutual respect and helpfulness, with recognition of the kind of contribution each can make to the purpose they share.

During these visits I became aware of the extent to which federal fund support adds quantity, variety and, in many instances, quality to privately sponsored programs; aware also that many projects would have to be discontinued or would be seriously crippled if government support were withdrawn. At the same time I saw no indication of blind (or bland) dependence on the public treasury (grants have already been too frequently delayed and too uncertain in amount to foster that condition). Evidence did not emerge of church-connected directors or staff members becoming "corrupted," "muted" or "cowed" by their OEO or other governmental relationships. I did find some dissatisfaction with what seemed to be "arbitrary," "unintelligent" or otherwise "objectionable" actions by the public grant agencies, about which complaints were registered directly with the agencies. Since the church project directors or associated denominational or council of churches leaders were frequently members of the local OEO agency, they could often remedy the situations or bring about better understanding of the problems.

About the spiritual implication of church-state relationships, most of these anti-poverty leaders would agree on one important point: The value of the churches' contribution to the social purpose of the poverty effort is of a magnitude that calls for well-considered, cooperative action by religious forces, utilizing such allies and such resources as are available—at the same time recognizing and accepting the calculated risks to the institutional church such actions may involve. I have the feeling that many of these people, fighting on the frontier of human need, would agree that the church's teaching about "losing one's life to find it" can have meaning for the church as an institution as well as for its individual members.

Changing Attitudes. Clearer and clearer, the farther I traveled, was the heavy burden carried by workers in poverty war projects in their unending struggle with the indifferent, cynical or just hopeless attitudes of many people with whom they deal. These negative attitudes are found *first* among the people in poverty whom they try to work for and with, and *next* among the people in plenty, both inside the churches and out, on whose understanding support the whole war depends.

Why are poor people often so hard to reach? I have never heard the answer more vividly stated than by Maryruth Nickels. Writing in the *Methodist Woman* (November, 1966), she says: "Poverty twists people mentally, morally and spiritually. . . . Many who dwell in slums live in a generalized state of fear of being attacked, robbed, bullied, knifed or having their children injured. This fear colors their whole lives: their ability to work, to learn, to stay healthy and sane, to venture out of their apartments or blocks, to live openly and freely, to be friends with their neighbors, and to trust outsiders, the world or themselves. Fear is a crippler in the slum."

Fear cripples many of us in many ways. Unless we have been desperately poor ourselves or lived in the midst of poverty, however, it is almost impossible to realize the extent to which it freezes people into withdrawing from other people and into looking with deep suspicion on any newcomer. Oppressed people are often willing to live with the status quo of their miserable condition because it is known to them, rather than to seek change where the process and outcome represent the unknown or uncertain.

A second attitude that comes between the anti-poverty worker and those needing help is deep personal apathy—again of an intensity al-

151

most unknown "outside." As Wilson C. McWilliams, perceptive writer in the *Saturday Review* (December 10, 1966), has seen it, "poverty is a feeling of personal unimportance." Added to fear is the pervading hopelessness that comes from never having been "off relief," of living one's whole childhood on a block where not one adult had a steady, family-supporting job, where "to be in poverty is to be entrapped . . . to be in a situation without choices, an environment without options."

These are the attitudes, built up through generations, that make many people in poverty areas slow to respond to the "option" of possible help or change; even slower to take up the "new and strange" opportunity for "maximum participation" in forbidding-looking boards and agencies. Confronting the blank wall of obstacles such as these explains why people of the churches—believed by many to be "the reservoir of the outpouring spirit"—are looked to especially for help.

The worthwhileness of the effort to help, no matter what it takes, comes through as one sees fear, apathy, hopelessness melt gradually under day-by-day exposure to the warming effects of outgiving human concern and helpfulness . . . when one hears a once-listless youngster returning from a go-see trip respond to the usual query with a glowing "Oh, I liked everything most!" . . . when one senses the momentous excitement of the migrant farm worker who, when signing her name in writing for the first time, cried "I am no longer an X, I am Mrs. Rosa Sanchez now."[3]

But how does one melt the even more frustrating misunderstanding or open hostility of those at the other end of the poverty worker's spectrum—the nonpoor?

Speaking facetiously but not unrealistically, one commentator has said that for 200 or 300 years Christians have told the world that all people are equal before God; "Now they're beginning to believe it and we're scared to death!" Dr. Carothers believes that "people stay poor because of the attitudes of the prosperous. . . ."

"The prosperous are the people who know that they have a continuing part in the larger community . . . they are the people who can buy on credit . . . they may not have much money on hand, but they have access to the flow of money, and they dip regularly into its stream. . . . In short, they feel that they are 'in' the main part of society and they know that they have rights (there) . . . they also tend to think that the poor do not deserve the same rights." In fact many holdover eighteenth and nineteenth century "myths" about why

[3] For more of this story and an excellent assessment of the goals and successes of the war to date, see William Lee Miller's article "I Am No Longer an X," *Together,* December 1966.

people are poor and what should be done about them cause honest but frequently uninformed people in and out of the churches to hamper or block church-dependent anti-poverty efforts.

Those working in poverty areas need support from the church members' influence as community decision makers. Every request to City Hall to extend a needed public service in a slum area or to a school board to replace a dilapidated school building is invariably considered by the responsible officials in terms of the attitudes of their constituents. Too often the "leading" citizens (frequently church people) turn out to be indifferent, totally uninformed about the conditions or openly hostile because "more taxes" may be involved. In many cases tax money would not be needed if public officials were stimulated by informed citizens—it usually doesn't take more than one, two or a small group—to do better what the laws and current budgets enable them to do. In other cases conditions are so flagrant that more tax money *should* be provided—willingly.

Still another important way the prosperous influence the lives of the poor is in the conscious or unconscious economic decisions "good" people make, particularly in the use of their money. As one long-experienced project director has cried out: "Who do you think owns the tenements, and gin mills, and whore houses in the neighborhoods where I work? Who operates the antiquated schools, perpetuates horribly inconsistent law enforcement, overlooks building-code violations, draws iron curtain boundaries of containment by gentlemen's agreements or by screaming expressways for the foot-bound poor in a mobile age. . . . Unless the voice of judgment is heard clearly in our land that that kind of so called 'rugged individualism' . . . is nothing more than plain inhuman greed, then the moral decay of our nation is almost complete."[4]

These hampering attitudes, on the part of both the impoverished and the prosperous, constitute serious, but not insurmountable, problems. The great poverty war contribution of the millions of church members who will not go to the battlefronts in the ghettos could be to become interested and informed about the conditions, needs and possibilities at these fronts and to use the powerful weapon of their personal influence where their attitudes and decisions count most—as citizens, property owners and investors.

OVERALL INFLUENCE OF RELIGIOUS FORCES

Evidences of the overall influence of religious forces, though not explicitly covered in this study, came to me in practically every city

[4] Kenneth Waterman, writing in *City Church*, November-December 1964.

or hamlet visited and are indicated directly or indirectly in many of the projects described.

Where leaders of a state or local council of churches or of a denomination were already active in community concerns, these men were commonly among the first to accept the immense challenge to local initiative offered by the federal anti-poverty program. In a few instances (such as in New Mexico) Protestant and Roman Catholic forces had already come together for cooperative action. In many more communities the need for across-the-board involvement of community forces in the poverty program brought the interchurch leadership together, for the first time, in close cooperation on issues and activities outside of traditional church boundaries. At many points influence and activity also became inter-religious as Jewish leaders and agencies joined their centuries-long concern with the efforts of the other religious forces.

Alongside the many pluses registered by the churches and church people during the first 2½ year anti-poverty struggle must be put also the negative weight of the vast, still unmoved iceberg of resistance, or more often indifference, that continues within the religious community. Some idea of its "tonnage" is indicated by a recent poll of attitudes toward their various functions taken among Protestant ministers by the National Council of Churches. A representative sampling of 5,600 clergy, including those of theologically conservative as well as liberal denominations, rated participation in community action fifteenth in importance among their ongoing activities. Working for neighborhood committees and other projects outside the church ranked last on the 22-item list. On my journeys I met none of the "typicals" in this sample group. I was continuously aware, however, of the many closed doors that could helpfully be opened along the way.

One other factor in overall influence is far less easy to pin down and write about. As I watched, listened and talked to many people at many points and from many angles, I became aware of an intangible something (a kind of essence I suppose), which seemed to pervade many of the person-to-person activities, attitudes or comments. References were made to "spiritual poverty," to "poverty of personality," to "problems that welfare checks alone will never solve," to "the magnificent potential reflected in a human face, once convinced that someone cares." From every side they told me: "Nothing like this ever happened to me before." "This is the most worthwhile thing I have ever done." "No one ever seemed to care 'til now." "It was the first time any one from a church ever came to our house."

Jan Gates, program director of Fellowship House in St. Louis, finally defined this something for me. In answer to my query as to how they had gained and maintained their obviously warm rapport with the people of every age and station, she said without hesitation, "It is a matter of relationship. In this kind of work there is just no substitute for *sustained love and trust.*"

. . . and there I had it—sustained love and trust—as old as time, as new as tomorrow . . . and still the most potent cement "close binding all mankind."

Providing two ingredients essential to the self-respect of the person in need and to mutual respect between the helper and the helped, I am convinced that this personal relationship is also the Ultimate Weapon, without which there never will be a successful war against poverty. Though the capacity for love and trust is in no sense unique to religiously motivated people, I found it to be an inherent element in most of the projects I visited and to account for much of their high quality of outreach to people in need and of inner stability of staff function and morale.

EVALUATION AND PERSPECTIVE ON THE FUTURE

William Lee Miller in his appraisal of the war in general concludes: "Against the background of Harlem and Harlan County, of Watts and Hough and Lowndes County, the federal war on poverty itself looks inadequate. But looked at with the realistic background of our past neglect and of the present reality of people helped, it looks very good, indeed."[5]

This I believe is true of the churches' effort as well. For one thing, by now nearly everyone knows we are fighting this war. More people and churches—more individuals and groups—are daily confronted with choices. They may still choose "out" instead of "in," but more people realize they are making a choice, and that in itself constitutes a substantial gain.

Many who are actually in this struggle see it not so much in terms of "the forest" of the total effort as of "the trees" of progress in individual lives reclaimed. One worker said to me, "In this war even if you lose you win, since every person 'developed' from dependence to indepedence or promise of it represents a victory in the Christian sense." From this viewpoint, successes have been and are being won in large numbers day by day in the projects visited. Multiplied manyfold, they constitute a steady build-up of three-way victories—for the person helped to new hope, for the person who helps make the hope

[5] *Op. cit.*

possible, for the many others involved in starting and maintaining the process as a whole.

"But can we really afford this war?" many people still ask. Perspective is offered by two recent items from fiscal sources. The first refers to the annual "fiscal dividend" which accrues to our federal tax system as a result of every increase in our Gross National Product (GNP), that is, as a result of steadily increasingly affluence. "Consider the magnitudes," says Dr. Dick Netzer, professor of public finance at the Graduate School of Public Administration, New York University, and then points out:

"Ten years from now, if federal tax rates remain unchanged federal revenues are likely to be $75-80 billion higher than they are now. If the experience of the past ten to fifteen years is repeated, the average annual increase to ordinary federal civilian expenditures will be less than $1.5 billion. Even if the current levels of federal civilian expenditures and grants were *doubled* over the next decade, *a substantial hypothetical fiscal dividend would remain to be distributed.*[6]

For the individual taxpayer who nearly always thinks he and his kind are "paying too much," my hometown newspaper has provided some perspective on the plight of the "poor rich folks" of Yonkers, New York. *The Herald Statesman* (February 2, 1967) reports that "according to Standard Rate and Data Service, the average Yonkers (family) income of $7,810 in 1956 has risen to $10,413 today." That compares favorably, says the reporter, with a Tax Foundation finding that "an American family making $7,500 in 1956 must be pulling in at least $8,825 today just to match the buying power of 10 years ago." So what the middle and upper income families are pulling in is not so bad. In fact, it is really very good, especially when the fact is added that this sizable city includes, in addition to its prosperous residents, a large number of below poverty line families as well. When this drag on the average income is lifted, the financial state of the above average family becomes even more impressive by contrast.

As has been said in numerous high places, we as a nation may choose not to fight until we have eliminated poverty from our midst, but if we do so choose, let us be sure that it is because of a lack of the will to do so on our part, and not because we think we cannot afford it financially, whether or not we are at the same time fighting a military war.

Regarding church groups, a large proportion of the individuals with

[6] "Proceed with a Plan" (for distribution of increasing federal revenues). *National Civic Review*, February 1967. (Italics added.)

steadily mounting incomes are among their most influential members. Here the choice to be made in the use of ever greater wealth, or potential, is again a matter of will and not of dollar resources.

Looking at the nation's, and our churches', effort of these first trial years as a whole, Rev. Shirley Greene, NCC's first Anti-Poverty Coordinator, has well summed up where we are and where we're going when he says:

"Poverty is now contrary to the public policy of the nation. I believe that once having made that declaration, we can never rescind it. However long the road and however fumbling may be our efforts, I am convinced that this country has established as a goal the elimination of poverty; and that we can never turn back now to the comfortable rationalizations of yesterday."[7]

We cannot do better than to move into the future with the realism and vision of the leaders of Westminster Neighborhood Association on the edge of Watts who say: *Our task is monumental, but we are not without hope.*

[7] "The Churches War Against Poverty." A sermon, National Council of Churches, 1965.

INDEX OF PROJECTS

A NOTE ABOUT THE FORMAT

Type: Caledonia 10 point leaded 2 points

Printed by: Sowers Printing Company, Lebanon, Pennsylvania

Typographic design by: Joan S. Cooper